ON PAUL HOLMER

ALSO AVAILABLE FROM BLOOMSBURY

Wittgenstein and Theology, Tim Labron

Science and Religion in Wittgenstein's Fly-Bottle, Tim Labron

Kierkegaard and Philosophical Eros: Between Ironic Reflection and Aesthetic Meaning, Ulrika Carlsson

Wittgenstein, Religion and Ethics: New Perspectives from Philosophy and Theology, ed. Mikel Burley

Authorship and Authority in Kierkegaard's Writings, ed. Joseph Westfall

ON PAUL HOLMER

A Philosophy and Theology

EDITED BY TIM LABRON

BLOOMSBURY ACADEMIC
LONDON • NEW YORK • OXFORD • NEW DELHI • SYDNEY

BLOOMSBURY ACADEMIC
Bloomsbury Publishing Plc
50 Bedford Square, London, WC1B 3DP, UK
1385 Broadway, New York, NY 10018, USA
29 Earlsfort Terrace, Dublin 2, Ireland

BLOOMSBURY, BLOOMSBURY ACADEMIC and the Diana logo
are trademarks of Bloomsbury Publishing Plc

First published in Great Britain 2023
This paperback published 2024
Copyright © Tim Labron, 2023

Tim Labron has asserted his right under the Copyright, Designs and
Patents Act, 1988, to be identified as Editor of this work.

Series design by Charlotte Daniels
Cover image: Sailor Rowing A Small Boat Through An Ocean Storm
(© John Lund / Getty Images)

All rights reserved. No part of this publication may be reproduced or
transmitted in any form or by any means, electronic or mechanical,
including photocopying, recording, or any information storage or
retrieval system, without prior permission in writing from the publishers.

Bloomsbury Publishing Plc does not have any control over, or responsibility for, any
third-party websites referred to or in this book. All internet addresses given in this
book were correct at the time of going to press. The author and publisher regret any
inconvenience caused if addresses have changed or sites have ceased to exist, but
can accept no responsibility for any such changes.

A catalogue record for this book is available from the British Library.

A catalog record for this book is available from the Library of Congress.

ISBN:	HB:	978-1-4725-9260-6
	PB:	978-1-3502-1487-3
	ePDF:	978-1-4725-9262-0
	eBook:	978-1-4725-9261-3

Typeset by Integra Software Services Pvt. Ltd.

To find out more about our authors and books visit www.bloomsbury.com
and sign up for our newsletters.

To Jake and Kyleah

CONTENTS

Posthumous Foreword The Rev. Dr. Eugene C. McDowell † viii

1 Paul Holmer and the Subject *Tim Labron* 1
2 Theology *Must* Be Projected *Brad J. Kallenberg* 37
3 Paul Holmer and the Religious Interpretation of Kierkegaard *Anders Kraal* 101
4 Paul Holmer and the Logic of Preaching *Jeffrey Willetts* 123
5 Paul Holmer and Theology as Grammar *Ryan Duerr* 171
6 Theology as Theosis *Terrance Klein* 197

Bibliography 228

Index 231

POSTHUMOUS FOREWORD

The Rev. Dr. Eugene C. McDowell †

I knew you briefly and you enriched me. Imagine the wealth for those who knew you longer.

Tim Labron

The afternoon I first walked into Paul Holmer's class I sensed an unusual energy. If I gave him a chance, this Paul Holmer might not only enhance my theological and philosophical thinking but might also somehow play a significant role in my becoming a more authentic human being.

That first day he invited the class, filled with budding theologians, to not simply look at theology but with theology. He also invited us, as we began our exploration within such a vast and marvelous university, to not lose sight of the God of Abraham, Isaac, and Jacob.

The three plus years I was his student, I thought new thoughts, dreamed new dreams, and considered new possibilities. With the aid of Soren Kierkegaard, Ludwig Wittgenstein, and others, I was encouraged by Professor Holmer to consider allowing a *capacity* to evolve in my life; a capacity that would allow me to love, serve, and praise God.

Holmer stayed a teacher and friend many years after my days at school. In doing so, he taught me to not take myself too seriously.

Many years ago I wrote and read a paper on trust at the American Academy of Religion. Since Holmer had not attended the meeting, I sent him a copy of my paper along with another article I had found written by a Stanford scholar. He wrote back: "Thank you for sending the papers. I found the one very insightful and helpful-not yours." He was wonderfully open and honest; one always knew where they stood, including other faculty and scholars. Almost forty years later, hardly a day goes by that I do not hear that strong, mid-western voice saying to his class; "In the end, true religion cannot be taught; it can only be caught." This and other simple yet powerful statements have urged my academic and church endeavors throughout my life.

I am most grateful to Professor Tim Labron for his work on Paul Holmer. I believe that his work captures the essence of the honest academic prowess, intellect, and wisdom of this unique and valuable theologian who continues to have so much to offer.

1

Paul Holmer and the Subject

Tim Labron

Brief Introduction

Paul Holmer is not particularly well known, and this is not very surprising. It is a result of his unique thought in contrast to the common and popular philosophical and theological trends. The latter popular thinking considers the point of philosophy and theology to build grand systems of thought or to facilitate building progressive social systems. He does not follow these modes of thought or trends and thereby appears to be much less interesting, less novel, less useful, etc., and therefore even perhaps pointless. Yet his thought, in contrast to whichever current trend, is timeless and particularly insightful.

In order to understand Holmer, it is natural to include some aspects of Kierkegaard, Wittgenstein, and C.S. Lewis. They were of great interest to Holmer and they naturally fit with his own thought. For example, his remark regarding Lewis can be directly related back to him: "one finds little about symbolism, ontology, and modern man in his literature. At first it may look as though he may not know about all this current thought and is simply being obtusely old-fashioned."[1] Additionally, "Lewis's thought is so different because it is not neatly separated into kinds and compartments,"[2] he is "singularly free of theories. ... His literary scholarship seems more calculated to improve the sensibility and to enlarge the capacities of the reader than it is to prove a thesis or to indicate a general outlook."[3] The same applies to Holmer's remarks on Kierkegaard: "To describe Kierkegaard's significance for theology has been made difficult rather than easy by the scholarship about him, for often he has been claimed to be ... anti-intellectual or too intellectual, anti-church or pro-Augustinian, too psychological or too theological or even both."[4] It is very common to misunderstand the thought of those who do not fit the usual pattern of the day, those who are not simply adding to the prevalent system building and social progress theories du jour.

I clearly do not presume to fully understand Holmer, and clearly cannot as skillfully address the issues at hand. In order to let Holmer speak on his own terms, I purposefully do not include a synopsis or cohesion of the writings within this book so that the reader may enter the following readings anew for him or herself and, as Wittgenstein would say, so the reader may do the work for him or herself and, as Holmer says: "The trick is not to be another's telos, but to let the telos arise in the other person. There must be knowledge first. But it must be so stated as to occasion a double reflection, a thought and the passion become what the thought pictures. This is all that one person can do for another in areas of most significance."[5]

Philosophy

Philosophy and theology continually attempt to answer fundamental questions. For example: "What is the Good?"; "What are the attributes of God?"; and ultimately, "What is the objectively true reality?" These types of questions are obviously asked by individuals, yet the search for answers very often purposefully attempts to leave the individual in the dust, and doing so is thought to engage serious academic thinking. For instance, we assume that we should discover the reality "out there" and we as individuals are, in a sense, quite passive and irrelevant in relation to the truths that are so sought. Granted, it is obvious that very generally speaking we can make sense of this point of view, there is a reality "out there" regardless of my existence and whatever I happen to think about it. However, the extent to which this objective point of view is taken for granted cannot be sustained and therefore requires discussion. That is, Holmer's point of view and correction.

The above so-called fundamental questions, that is the ethico-religious, and even scientific, cannot as is typically assumed be answered in a categorically objective manner—one's participation as a subject is a necessary ingredient. Such a seemingly brash idea will immediately lead many to think that what is then being suggested is subjectivism, emotivism, relativism, postmodernism, etc.; but such a cursory conclusion is simply the result of being caught in the net of what Holmer calls the "intellectual myth"; namely, the problem of placing passion and subjectivity on the one hand, and detachment and objectivity on the other, in a strict opposition to one another. This is the conceptual trap of this intellectual myth; namely, wrongly assuming the former to be good since it effectively eliminates the latter. The foundation of the myth is that "truth" and "reality" cannot include an individual's passion and subjectivity (at best they are a subsequent connection), and instead "truth" and "reality" are a grand "something" beyond dynamic individuals in order to maintain objectivity—which is assumed to be largely secure and static. Once again, this strict objectivity has obvious relevance and is not outright wrongheaded; the problem is the extent to which it is taken.

As Holmer notes, "By always thinking big and forgetting oneself, one can easily get the reputation of being concerned with the transcendent and massive 'real' issues. By calling all such concerns a preoccupation with reality, one has an almost invulnerable position."[6] Indeed, it has become an unquestionable tenant of thought; namely, the pursuit of truth and objectivity is honorable while anything including subjectivity and the individual is suspect. This is, according to Holmer, the wrong way to proceed. He notes Kierkegaard saying:

> [M]odern philosophy has tried anything and everything in the effort to help the individual to transcend himself objectively, which is a wholly impossible feat; existence exercises its restraining influence, and if philosophers nowadays had not become mere scribblers in the service of fantastic thinking and its preoccupation, they would long ago have perceived that suicide was the only tolerable practical interpretation of its striving.[7]

Moreover, Holmer rightly notes, regarding Kierkegaard, that "all such elaborate conceptual shifts were only done by philosophers and were a kind of elaborate legerdemain. It comes of pretending that one can think *sub specie eternatatis*, and, again, the only cure is to remember that one is not all-knowing or the Absolute."[8] The common point of view of placing the individual and subjectivity on the side while inflating one's cognitive abilities creates a very odd conception of knowledge.

On the one hand, the individual and subjectivity are belittled, while on the other hand, the individual's thinking is inflated to be able to transcend themselves, that is, humanity, to the expanse of metaphysical and universal truths. In contrast, Holmer strives to show the significance of the individual's subjectivity. Of course, this does not mean that Holmer outright rejects the categories of objective and subjective, instead he clarifies them. Moreover, his point is not epistemological—it is logical. He is not interested in how one's seemingly hidden and distant brain comes to have knowledge of the external and separate truths "out there." Correspondingly, he notes regarding Lewis that he "is not repudiating the quest for knowledge, nor the insatiable curiosity that wants to know. His thesis is a logical one. It is, briefly, that general laws do not and cannot explain human behaviour."[9] The key is not arguing within the typical characterization of objective and subjective, to find such general laws or theories regarding our knowledge of things, but to see the logic of objective and subjective, and the individual's role in this dynamic interaction when discussing the ethico-religious.

Think of ethics for a moment, and asking "what is the Good?" It is sometimes thought that the key concern is to discern the objective universal truth of the Good, then once it is known action may follow, in a type of causal relationship. If we know what the good is we can then apply it to humanity. To do so, we assume the best way forward is to remove oneself in favor of the universal Good beyond individuals, and to reason toward and even perhaps identify with the universal Good. Plato, for one, set us on the unproductive task of seeking the object "Good," however the "Good" is not an object to be discovered. For instance, asking "what is the Good?" is clearly different from asking "what is sea salt?" Confusion results from mistakenly using the same grammar for "sea salt" and "Good" as if they are grammatically analogical—again a logical point, not an epistemological point. Thus, abstractly asking "what is the Good?" is vacuous since our concept of the Good is then abstracted into a realm with no clear application.

Of course, this does not mean that there is no good and, on the other hand, that there is no evil, that all is simply relative, which would be a very cursory conclusion. The common assumption that we need to determine the objective Good leads to the notion that any critique of objectivity is simply wrong since it shifts toward a woolly subjectivity. According to Holmer, this is not surprising. He rightly notes regarding Lewis: "we are so accustomed to highly contrived accounts of moral life and to having our thoughts everlastingly described as objective if we are having to do with facts and subjective if we are considering values, that we can scarcely gather in the drift of his ideas."[10] Again, rather than actually working through Holmer's thought to understand him, it is more common to dismiss his thought—it is easier.

This continual search for the objective "Good" beyond our multifaceted world in the metaphysical realm where the unchanging truth is lurking continues the intellectual myth. This mythical point of view is very wide based and, for comparison, even finds an analogy in mathematics. Yet, mathematics must also be grammatically correct (logical) in contrast to being epistemologically correct. For example, is a mathematical formula directed toward an object? S.G. Shanker notes that one who believes this to be the case, namely that mathematics deals with existing entities, "has not strayed unawares into some unexpected domain; he has deliberately ventured into the void because like Jason he thinks he can return with the Golden Fleece, if only he has sufficient courage and perseverance."[11] An example of this mathematical flight is found in Max Tegmark's theory, his "Mathematical Universe Hypothesis," specifically that a mathematical monism exists and thereby mathematical entities exist.[12] Although Wittgenstein is not commenting on Tegmark in particular, he aptly notes:

> [T]he comparison with alchemy suggests itself. We might speak of a kind of alchemy in mathematics. It is the earmark of this mathematical alchemy that mathematical propositions are regarded as statements about mathematical objects, – and so mathematics as the exploration of these objects. In a certain sense it is not possible to appeal to the meaning of the signs in mathematics, just because it is only mathematics that gives them their meaning.[13]

In this case, as with others, there is an attempt to deal with things posited that "exist," but they only exist because they are thought. Mathematical formulations, and the Good, do not exist as standalone entities, yet it is not uncommon to find various theories removed from the world to formulate an abstract certainty, to evade any potential uncertainty. However, among many things, mathematics and the Good are only understood in multifaceted applications.

Whether it is philosophy, theology, or mathematics, the search the "Golden Fleece" fits Holmer's comment: "intelligent people confront the uncertainties of life with all kinds of talents. Some of them complicate matters by seeing the uncertainties as temporary gaps in an otherwise seamless robe of complete truth, and one is intimidated by the gallantry of the vision."[14] Or, as he notes Kierkegaard saying, the "intelligent man proposes 'another understanding', or he searches out the 'meaning', or he discerns another 'reality' which will change the logical case rather more favorably."[15] These attempts are confused since the concepts dealt with are not actually reality concepts. They exit the individual's life toward an illusionary objectified metaphysical dream.

Once again, those who follow the myth assume that any point of view other than the myth endorses relativism, wild subjectivity, and has no regard for serious thinking and the truth. As Paul Holmer says, "metaphysical distinctions were couched in language that emerged exhaustive of the possibilities, thus the idealist/realist distinction does not appear to leave any middle ground."[16] In contrast, he notes favorably that Lewis "forged a conception of what theories and people were such that the logic of indecision, or relativism, of countless incompatibilities was bypassed altogether."[17] Nonetheless, as Wittgenstein says, "the very things which are most obvious may become the hardest of all to understand. What has to be overcome is a difficulty having to do with the will, rather than the intellect."[18] Holmer wants to show that there is a logical point, not an epistemological or metaphysical investigation at stake. Yet his logical point can be easily missed, and instead his thought may be superficially labeled as unremarkable, that he is missing the metaphysical earnestness of a theory, or such; anything to avoid trying to work on his thought as it stands. Anything to avoid, as Wittgenstein says, working through one's "will."

For example, it is clear that Wittgenstein in his "later" work was dealing with a logical point rather than an epistemological point. As D.Z. Phillips says, regarding Wittgenstein's "later" work and philosophical point that he wants to bring out "the kind of questions they are—that they are questions in logic, not questions in epistemology."[19] The superficial reader of Wittgenstein will reply that this is nonsense since in Wittgenstein's early work there was a great deal of work on logic, much more so than his later work. Superficially this is true, yet it entirely misses the depth of Wittgenstein's later logical point—one that Holmer did grasp. Additionally, Holmer finds that Kierkegaard is also focused on logical points[20] and that Lewis's logic is "powerful."[21] The question is not whether or not Holmer, Wittgenstein, and Lewis, deal with logic, instead it is whether or not the reader has the will to work through to see the logical point.

For example, consider the logic of a stone exists. Some have built epistemological grounds regarding the relation between one's ideas and the stone through the use of the notions of sense-data, primary and secondary qualities such as shape and size and color, and then how these turn into ideas in one's brain, etc., to explain how we know that there is a stone in front of us. Given the rather convoluted path of various theories and qualities from the external stone to one's so-called internal ideas suggested, for example by Locke, led Berkeley to conclude that it is impossible to make the connection between an external physical stone and one's idea of the stone, therefore the stone is in our brain existing as an idea. Of course, given the serious philosophical thinking put into showing how there actually is a stone or it is just an idea, and whatever other theories there may be, Holmer readily notes Kierkegaard's apt point: "the humor of all this lies in the assumption that philosophy provides proofs for the learned where the ignorant can only believe."[22]

The notion of an inner self with a potential cognitive ability which is a passive recipient of sense data is a misleading picture.

We need to get rid of this epistemological misconception of the individual. As Holmer remarks:

> One picture, a crudely intellectualized one, is misleading and falsifying. It would picture the self as a *tabula rasa*, receiving the "sensations," synthesizing them, focussing ideas, testing them in relation to things, and issuing finally in judgments ... Then the objectivities would be met by a judging intellect, who then would so formulate an account of what is the case, that subjectivity would follow as a matter of course.[23]

The problem here is the clear separation between the inner self and the external objective reality. Certainly, all will say that there is a self to receive external data, there is some connection, yet the connection is clearly and frequently regarded as a causal connection of categorically objective data causally input into one's brain with no account of subjectivity. Indeed, it is often thought that subjectivity gets in the way of the data input!

In contrast, what is emphasized by Holmer is the need to take into account the role of the individual and subjectivity as something other than a receptor of casual data, as he notes Kierkegaard saying, "It depends then, not only on what a man sees, but what a man sees depends upon how he sees it. For observing is not only a receiving or a discovery for it is also a matter of bring something forward; and in so far as it is that, the crucial matter becomes what the observer himself is."[24] It is arguable to note that philosophers and theologians in particular have difficulties with seeing this active role of the individual and subjectivity—as not simply the entity receiving external truths. Holmer rightly states, words "are not coins with their values stamped on their surfaces. We are led to this mistake by the notion that words are defined, that we look up their meanings in dictionaries, that they are thus public while our feelings, loves, and quickening stay private."[25] In other words, "reality" is not categorically something "out there" that a passive individual, like any other passive individual, discovers; instead, there is an interplay between each individual and reality.

Interestingly, post-classical physics, and quantum theory in particular—albeit clearly a different context—is working with this very notion. This is a seemingly odd situation, the often assumed "soft" thought of metaphysical philosophy and theology rejecting the participatory nature of the subject in contrast to the "hard" thought of physics which includes the individual's participation in reality. It is thereby useful for comparison to briefly include some thoughts from the domain of physics.

For example, Anton Zeilinger remarks, "while in the classical worldview, reality is a primary concept prior to and independent of observation with all its properties, in the emerging view of quantum mechanics the notions of reality and of information are on equal footing."[26] Moreover, he notes Wolfgang Pauli writing:

> To me it seems quite adequate to call the conceptual description of nature in classical physics ... the ideal of the detached observer. In drastic words the spectator must, according to this ideal, appear in a fully discrete manner as a hidden spectator. He can never appear as an actor. Nature is hereby left alone in its predetermined course of events, without regard to the manner in which the phenomena are observed.[27]

Additionally, as Giambattista Vico observed, long before Kierkegaard and this discovery in physics, the "complementarity [between the subjective and objective] issues forth not from rationalistic pseudo-unity of intellectual categories but rather from an organic unity derived from the phenomena of its very origins."[28]

Although obvious, it needs to be made clear that it is not the case in physics that the observer imagines something and then consequently this individual's subjectivity exclusively makes something become "real," rather it is the case that the observer's participation in measurement determines along with physical reality the result (e.g., a particles position). So, just as the point in physics includes an active observer along with physical reality, not a wildly random subjectivity, the same point applies to Holmer pointing out the significance of a participating subjectivity, but not one that fabricates a willy-nilly reality.

The organic nature of the necessary tie to nature and our lives rather than an abstract theoretical system forms a better understanding of reality in contrast to further abstractions and ratiocinations, as further noted by Zeilinger regarding the need for conceptual clarification: "I do not mean an axiomatic formalization of the mathematical foundations of quantum mechanics, but a foundational conceptual principle."[29] Likewise, Holmer states that Kierkegaard's "aim is to help clear up conceptual confusions that have been accrued, not to further formalize them."[30]

Neither Kierkegaard nor Holmer want to build another theory, they want to show the logic of concepts in our everyday lives, and to show the vacuous nature of the empty essences, entities, etc., posited by metaphysics. The point is not to formalize or extend conceptual troubles beyond our lives but to place concepts in our lives and at work.

For example, Holmer states: "Kierkegaard found that though the concepts of the possible, the actual, and the probable all had objective reference, they did not name powers in nature. Probability is not an objective force working in events. Therefore, he tries valiantly to make his reader see that it is a concept, not a name."[31] Likewise, Wittgenstein read Hertz and said that he "addresses the problem of how to understand the mysterious concept of force as it is used in Newtonian physics. Hertz proposes that, instead of giving a direct answer to the question: 'what is force?', the problem would be dealt with by restating Newtonian physics without using 'force' as a basic concept. When these painful contradictions are removed, he writes, 'the questions as to the nature of force will not have been answered, but our minds, no longer vexed, will cease to ask illegitimate questions.'"[32] It is a given that there are concepts, yet the conceptual trouble is wrongly thinking that there is a universal that is therein named, when in fact there is no concept *qua* concept without subjectivity's activity in life. The logic in play here is one of participation, in contrast to abstract metaphysical ideals.[33] The logic of terms is not determined by reference alone or metaphysical categories, which can be an epistemological issue, but logically through the interplay within life. As Holmer states, "'Reality' words and concepts are all achievement words. They are not names."[34]

Thus, Wittgenstein rightly says that there is a "Remarkable and characteristic phenomena in philosophical investigation: the difficulty—I might say—is not that of finding the solution but rather of recognizing as the solution something that looks as if it were only preliminary to it ... This is connected, I believe, with our wrongly expecting an explanation, if we give it the right place in our considerations. If we dwell upon it, and do not try to get beyond it. The difficulty here is: to stop."[35]

Likewise, as Holmer notes Lewis saying: "you cannot go on 'explaining away' forever: you will find that you have explained explanation itself away. You cannot go on 'seeing through' things forever. The whole point of seeing through something is to see something through it. ... To 'see through' all things is the same as not to see."[36]

We analyze so much without even thinking about it, as Holmer rightly says that we often turn everything into a "this is what it means" as if the concept behind an event is superior to the event itself:

> It is as if then a logic of a situation, of a state of affairs, is finally being broached. And we are no longer wallowing in points of views and perspectives. Once we become accustomed to no longer looking at literature, or for that matter, at the facts around us, always trying to discern their hidden law or their potent, we are free to let the world and poems do their more fundamental job upon us. Then the logic of the world, the morphology of things the way they are, can really be received.[37]

Again, as Wittgenstein notes, do we have the will to see?

The point here is to stop explaining beyond the activity and participation, and instead use the practice and measurement at hand. To so proceed is to understand the ethico-religious, to move from empty concepts and an inflated notion of objectivity of the "intellectual myth" toward an understanding of subjectivity with the concept of truth as subjectivity. Yet, once again, it cannot be emphasized enough that this does not mean that the opposite is then the answer, namely that we must avoid objectivity and bask in the light of pure subjectivity—certainly not. The rantings of a lunatic enclosed in oneself are not a dialectic with the truth! As Holmer notes: "truth as subjectivity does not represent an aesthetic intuition or a poetic surmise; it is not an undialetical intuition nor a revelation from God. Neither is it an immediately apparent or self-evident truth. ... It presupposes objective warrantability."[38] In other words, subjectivity is not privacy, and there is a logic in truth as subjectivity.

That truth is subjectivity rids us of the wrongheaded concept that there is, for example, a religious or ethical "truth" that is simply a link with an "objective" truth, and thereby stops the wrongheaded questions and consequent answers. There is objective truth, for example the concept that truth is subjectivity, but the truth therein is not the truth described. What is required is the individual's action. Just as Bohr's point is that we cannot have new information beyond the experiments, we can only show the results of the experiments. It is the subjects' activity that engages truth rather than truth being an objective stricture which the subject apprehends, and the warrantability is in the practice.

Given complementarity and saying "truth is subjectivity," one may wonder how anything is actually determined. Is it all chance, a roll of the dice? Is the point simply a chaos? Are there no ethical truths? It is common in philosophy to assume that propositions must refer to truth (or they are false) and have a meaning in and of themselves, consequently many readers will be baffled with Holmer's thought since it seems to criticize others yet not develop an alternative template for reality or a "better" theory. The point, however simple yet at the same time difficult to grasp, is that the relation with truth is not simply between an ethical or religious proposition and an objective state of affairs, but a proposition and one's own life. In other words, as Holmer says, "Here language begins to be part of a form of life and it is not about it."[39]

Consider, again, the good. The point is to see that the good is not something to be put into a box and conceptualized, instead it is that which we see through discussions of ethics and living, it is in that account, not outside of it. The problem of viewing the good as a foundational abstract category is that it makes it seem as if it is more good, so to speak, than a good action. Just as Plato thought that the Good and, for example, geometric forms are fundamentally ideal existing entities, in contrast to our misaligned world.

There is a continual drive to find the system or theory that is, in some way, superior to our shifting world and certain, yet uncertainty is what drives the living subject. As Holmer notes, "We have seen the temptations. One kind of philosophy, idealism, makes the forms and ideas into realities, and then the issue of synthesis cannot arise and there is no uncertainty about reality. Another kind of philosophy construes idealities, whether sensations, ideas, or logical values, simply as reals, and again there can be no objective uncertainty."[40] Incidentally, the parallel here to physics is what is called the information paradox, that is, that a black hole just might be swallowing information into oblivion, if so, those physicists who fear uncertainty are afraid that this may take away physical law and make reality indeterminate.

When the good is not abstracted into a metaphysical object it draws on distinctions as primary, it draws on the particular. The point is that the good is not something that is simply known prior to practice in life—it is formed in life. Holmer rightly notes that "Kierkegaard is against an objective ethic because it tries to state what ethical men 'believe', 'while' or 'before' they behave."[41] We do not think a concept and then mechanically apply it, rather we use them within concrete actions. Furthermore, no one can do all things, so there is no one concept of the good and, in any case, even if all knowledge was certain there would still be uncertainty in its use. The point is that the individual is faced with possibilities and given these possibilities will decide upon a course of action, not through proofs, but convictions.

To understand the course of action and convictions is to see what Kierkegaard calls the subject's passion. However, the intellectualist myth confuses passions and concepts by juxtaposing them as opposites. Indeed, "The learned can often mask their lives in impressive talk that is not quite their own and within which they do not actually negotiated their lives."[42] Thus, "He must reflect his way out of the intellectualizing and back into his passions, out of the interesting and back into the simple." Thus, philosophy is "not to provide the proofs but really to energize the subject once again."[43] Philosophy is an activity, not a subscription to analytic doctrines.

While the intellectual myth assumes that an objective conceptualization of the "good" is primary, Holmer contrastingly and rightly agrees with Kierkegaard, namely "he would have us remember that being a human is not to be already a subject; it is to be so constituted that we make ourselves into subjects."[44] The good is not a matter of premises and conclusions. To assume that this is the case is to wrongly construe the logic of the discussion. That is, the subject is not a receptor of ethico-religious "truths," instead the subject is a passionate participant with choices.

As such, Kierkegaard points to the importance and "duty of existing," and it is this duty that leads Holmer to remark that "Reality for Kierkegaard is an ethical issue." If the subject were simply a machine that receives data, like a computer, and then causally moves according to that data, then the subject is very indifferent indeed: emotions against an algorithm and rationality. In contrast, we do not simply examine and input "reality," instead it, so to speak, examines us and expects a passionate response.

Further, Holmer notes that "the point is, I believe, that Lewis has seen in all of this that the self is both a recipient of a host of things and also an active agent. More properly, the self is a relation, not a thing."[45]

It is clear that an argument is not being made by Holmer to prove a particular ethico-religious point of view, to provide epistemological foundations, or build a metaphysical system. Since these are not the aims, many will be baffled regarding his position. In short, it is that none of these ways of supposedly progressing are actually progressing; in contrast, the logical point must be seen, that is, the logic of the ethico-religious. Of course, then the question will be, "what is this logic?" To this end, it is helpful to provide an example through theology.

Theology

It is clear that most agree that when we talk about rocks there are actual rocks, planets, and so on, regardless of the epistemological theory one holds (of course, excluding some form of idealism). However, when religion is the topic there is clearly a distinction. Some will say nothing of the sort exists, such as God and spirits, while others say such things do exist. The former posit that any such beliefs are, for example, just subjective delusions or emotive hopes, and in any case a primitive form of thinking. Holmer himself states: "Because we share a kind of positivism or a kind of naturalism, really mostly an attitude and, in some cases, only a theory, we tend to postulate this realm of neutral and given facts.... [and then] religious dogmas, poetry, morals and emotion to the value side and hence, subjectivity."[46] Again, subjectivity is derided in contrast to a clear objectivity. Yet Holmer rightly notes, regarding Lewis, that those for whom "skepticism and antifaith talk is all due to increasing maturation, new discoveries, better understanding, and general improvement in the race—all of that Lewis finds to be false."[47]

The following discussion is not meant to address whether or not there is a God. Rather it is to show the nature of the ethico-religious. Yet it is useful to note Holmer's comment: "It is the supposed factual reference that has made religious sentences appear to be crypto-scientific and hence occasioned repeated conflicts between science and religion ... both religious apologists and attackers have shared this genial error in the past, thus exciting glee that was incommensurate with either the proofs or the refutations."[48] In other words, it is common for both the atheist and the religious apologist to formulate the same form of questions and the consequence is, of course, wrongheaded answers. Again, a confusion between the logic of factual reference and the ethico-religious is being maintained in favor of the "intellectual myth."

Holmer points out that "Soon everything becomes a position, a point of view, a hypothesis or a problem; for these are the coin of the academic realm."[49] Consequently, Holmer notes, "I am bold enough to suggest that recent theology is positively amateurish on these matters."[50] Why? Because, it is amateurish when dealing with the ethico-religious and falls into the "intellectual myth," and this myth fears objective uncertainty, even though objective uncertainty is the nature and logic of the ethico-religious. Indeed, Holmer notes that whatever takes away this uncertainty is a superstition.[51]

Holmer wants us to move from the epistemological to the logic of the ethico-religious. Again, this is not a matter of formalization in logical terms, just as Wittgenstein's later work is in particular making a logical point—despite not using logical formalization. Instead, the point is deeper, to show that the "logic of ethico-religious discourse is different than the logic of much scholarly discourse."[52] For instance, Holmer says that "Historical statements and religious statements are in two different logical genres."[53] Moreover, he remarks:

> "Kierkegaard saw that empiricism, with its absorption in the explanation and description of natural facts, was incorrigibly abstract and remote from ethico-religious issues as was any speculative idealism. Furthermore, the logic of empirical thought and the categories and concepts thereof were as irrelevant to moral and religious discourse as were those conceived by speculative idealist philosophers."[54]

Consider the Bible. Just as the "Good" is not an object nor is God an object, so the Bible is not a set of true propositions about this object.[55] Again, many will retort, "but there is a God!" and "the Bible is true!" Such a reply is the consequence of holding on to the "intellectual myth." In no manner is it suggested that there is no God or that the Bible is a false document. As Holmer notes regarding Kierkegaard, that he "does not deny metaphysics all meaning simply because he denies that thought and reality are one. Nor does he deny the objectivity of Jesus, of actual existence, of the canons of thought, simply because he notes the importance of subjectivity and the difficulties of the ontological logic of his day."[56]

Many side step the obvious case that tautological truths are certain as a consequence of removing them, as it were, from the world; while the empirical entails the world and consequently change and the possibility of hypotheses. The result of this is turning God into an empirical hypothesis as an object. Yet neither the "good" nor God is either probable or improbable. Thus, Holmer notes that Kierkegaard "never says that a Christian should not say that the scriptures are the absolute truth. But the concept of truth is the issue. His point is that the fundamentalist-like belief in the truth of Scripture is also a confusion, however strong it seems religiously."[57] In brief, the point is that an epistemological approach to the Bible, a "fundamentalist-like belief," pursues studies to ensure the truth of the matter but cannot, in principle, reach a definitive conclusion, while at the same time those who believe the Bible to be God's Word are rightly certain. Given this certainty, and still holding on to the "intellectual myth," results in a discord between, for example, historical facts and this very certainty.

Given the nature of seeking objective certainty for the Bible, Holmer could see that inspiration was just a theory to deal with the problematic epistemological fact checking and patch up the holes. That is, "Attempts of religious thinkers to make all the sentences of religious literature both factual and certain led to such absurdities as inspiration and infallibility, both desperate efforts to make secure what could not in fact be made secure."[58] Thus, inspiration was taken as a formalization dealing with true facts, but by proceeding in such a manner its focus was on the myth and not the content. As theologian Herman Sasse notes: "It was a mistake... when theologians thought they could prove and demonstrate the truth of the scripture by setting it forth as the most perfect book, as a great, complete, contradictionless system of absolutely pure truths, absolutely true statements. It is not a system of statements, that is philosophy's conception of truth."[59] The Bible is made to appear, given the above, as a text that exists prior to religion, perhaps even on analogy to a Platonic form.

In contrast, Holmer notes regarding the Bible, that "it is not that special organs of knowing are at work or a particular kind of epistemic insightfulness presupposed. Rather there is a precision, not so much of feeling and emotions, but of description. Besides, there is an uninhibited use of everyday language ... Such literature is also remarkably theory-free and all the better for that."[60] From another perspective, the Bible does not teach the world view of the historical authors, it uses them, and in turn, it is to be used today, not proven.

Just as some wrongly consider the Bible to be a book of truths within an epistemological context, others likewise continue along the lines of this "intellectual myth" by regarding sermons to be in the business of stating true propositions. However, Kierkegaard notes that a sermon's "aim is not the 'truth.'"[61] Again, some may react by saying, "wait, sermons are full of truths!" However, Kierkegaard's point obviously is not that a sermon is necessarily full of falsehoods. Again, such a remark is the consequence of maintaining the "intellectual myth." Holmer rightly says, "The peculiarity of the religious act of faith ... is that it requires not simply that I hold certain sentences to be true, but rather that I am becoming the possibility thus described."[62] Again, the point is a living participation in contrast to a subscription to a theory, and the result is found in Holmer's remark on Kierkegaard: "Where most authors are pedestrian and flat-footed and at best can repeat biblical rubrics with only slight elaboration, Kierkegaard can both illustrate in his own person and sketch for his reader the dramaturgical feature of Christian inwardness."[63] Yet this does not mean that as an alternative Holmer recommends a vague sense of love, as he says, "speaking the truth in love is not relevant if all we have to offer is general advice and a kind of tacky mishmash of current psychology, everyday observation, and moralistic policy recommendations."[64]

Just as understanding the Bible and sermons as dealing in "truths" is regarded as wrongheaded by Holmer, he finds a similar problem within theological application. That is, applications that also try to replace the subject just as inspiration did, but in this case with what may be regarded as the true, so to speak, outward and objective social plan. He notes that "scholars and scientists are easily motivated to turn ethical and religious convictions into hypotheses or generalizations and thus seek their certification in the public domain."[65]

Here, it is not inspiration that is the glue to "fix" epistemological troubles, now it is the public implementation that is the focus. So, the individual subject is again removed in order to gain respectable solid ground. Clearly these are different contexts, yet the same point remains. The former replaces subjectivity with inspiration and the latter replaces subjectivity with societal implementation. The public concern also removes the individual in terms of responsibility since, as Holmer says, "If we allow ourselves to be caught up in the popular concern about solving all the social problems of the day, we will soon come to believe that poverty, ignorance, and social deprivation are the worst evils."⁶⁶ While the real evil, as it were, is with and in the individual subject, not an abstract society.

Consequently, as the individual is removed, Holmer notes: "a kind of political-social gentility has developed. That very gentility, which appears to be serene and non-ideological, above all strife and labels, gets to be the spirituality of the intellectuals and near-intellectuals. This is like a liberal and non-theological kind of religiosity."⁶⁷ This amounts to an abstraction from the individual to a societal form. Perhaps one can say a working toward the righteousness of society in contrast to the individual. In any case, as Holmer notes:

> Our difficulty in understanding the Gospel lies in the strange consequences of this conformity on our part. For we soon learn to be modern, to be always contemporary. We make a skill of keeping up. The world around us rewards rather showily for assimilating the day's news, newspapers, cheap books, radio, and TV—all of these surround us with information ... A situation of dependency grows up. We begin to think that that our daily existence and the very shape of our lives is a function of that maelstrom that whirls around us.⁶⁸

That is, forgetting oneself and replacing oneself with external and transient happenings. Furthermore, as Lewis sarcastically notes, "What we want if men are to become Christian at all, is to keep them in the state of mind I call Christianity and the New Psychology, Christianity and the New Order, ... Christianity and Vegetarianism, Christianity and Spelling Reform. If they must be Christian let them at least be Christians with a difference. Substitute for the faith itself some Fashion with a Christian colouring."[69]

As continually noted, if there is not a metaphysical system, objective true facts, or societal programs, to prove and provide legitimacy for faith, then what is substance of faith? The answer is to exit the "intellectual myth" and live faith. This is clearly not an epistemological or metaphysical argument, and thereby Holmer clearly understands the difficulty of this realization. As Holmer notes, "This surely is an occasion for not being able to go on. For if that is the way it is, then Christianity indeed looks out of step with the most advanced thinking as well as concerned social planning."[70]

Thus, Holmer states that "The pretensions of philosophers and aesthetes, on the one hand, and the ineptness and religious grossness of the Church, on the other, were both a reflection of a forgetfulness of what human life really is, and consequently also a misuse of concepts and propositions about religious and ethical matters."[71]

Given such abstractions that remove the individual, Holmer states: "All of those who, impressed by the engines of society and anxious to secure conformity to God, country, and duty, and who have slandered man by taking the adventure away—these are Kierkegaard's foes. That they include the clerics too, he was quick to note."[72] Rather than working within the "intellectual myth" to secure the objective truth of religious propositions or the "right" societal plan which take away "adventure," the point is to be an adventure, that is, an individual in progress. Yet an objective pursuit is much easier since it dissolves the individual and turns that which is sought into a will-o-the-wisp. As Holmer states, "*cognitively* men do not encounter a divine being."[73]

Notes

1 Paul Holmer, *C.S. Lewis: The Shape of His Faith and Thought* (New York: Harper & Row, 1976), 6.

2 Ibid., 61.

3 Ibid., 13.

4 Paul Holmer, *The Paul L. Holmer Papers: Thinking the Faith with Passion*, ed. David J. Gouwens and Lee C. Barett III (Cambridge: James Clarke & Co, 2013), 42.

5 Paul Holmer, *The Paul L. Holmer Papers: On Kierkegaard and the Truth*, ed. David J. Gouwens and Lee C. Barett III (Cambridge: James Clarke & Co, 2013), 258.

6 Holmer, *C.S. Lewis*, 43–4.

7 Holmer, *The Paul L. Holmer Papers: On Kierkegaard and the Truth*, 125.

8 Ibid., 211.

9 Holmer, *C.S. Lewis*, 25.

10 Ibid., 59.

11 S.G. Shanker, *Wittgenstein and the Turning-Point in the Philosophy of Mathematics* (New York: State University of New York, 1987), 288.

12 Max Tegmark, *Our Mathematical Universe: My Quest for the Ultimate Nature of Reality* (New York: Knopf, 2014), 53.

13 Ludwig Wittgenstein, *Remarks on the Foundations of Mathematics*, ed. G.H. von Wright, Rush Rhees, and G.E.M. Anscombe (Oxford: Basil Blackwell, 1978), 142e.

14 Holmer, *The Paul L. Holmer Papers: On Kierkegaard and the Truth*, 165.

15 Ibid., 145.

16 Ibid., 158.

17 Holmer, *C.S. Lewis*, 23.

18 Ludwig Wittgenstein, *Culture and Value*, ed. G.H. von Wright in collaboration with Heikki Nyman, trans. Peter Winch (Chicago, IL: University of Chicago Press, 1984), 17.

19 D.Z. Phillips (ed.), *Wittgenstein's on Certainty: There—Like Our Life* (Oxford: Blackwell, 2005), 135.

20 Holmer, *The Paul L. Holmer Papers: On Kierkegaard and the Truth*, 63.

21 Holmer, *C.S. Lewis*, 13.

22 Ibid., 225.

23 Holmer, *C.S. Lewis*, 88.

24 Holmer, *The Paul L. Holmer Papers: On Kierkegaard and the Truth*, 111.

25 Holmer, Paul, *The Paul L. Holmer Papers: Communicating the Faith Indirectly*, ed. David J. Gouwens and Lee C. Barett III (Cambridge: James Clarke & Co, 2013), 16.

26 Anton Zeilinger, "A Foundational Principle for Qunatum Mechanics," *Foundations of Physics*, 29, no. 4 (1999), 642.

27 Anton Zeilinger, "Vastakohtien todellisuus," in *Festschrift for K. V. Laurik Ainen*, ed. U. Ketvel et al. (Helsinki: Helsinki University Press, 1996), 174.

28 Emanuel L. Paparella, *Hermeneutics in the Philosophy of Giambattista Vico: Vico's Paradox; Revolutionary Humanistic Vision for the New Age* (San Francisco: EMText, 2003), 47.

29 Zeilinger, "A Foundational Principle for Qunatum Mechanics," 631.

30 Holmer, *The Paul L. Holmer Papers: On Kierkegaard and the Truth*, 36.

31 Ibid., 187.

32 Ray Monk, *Ludwig Wittgenstein: The Duty of Genius* (London: Jonathan Cape, 1990). Wittgenstein quoted in Monk, 26.

33 Additionally, it should not be a surprise to anyone to know that mathematics alone when used to workout various astronomical features does not provide any clear understanding unless tied to a computer simulation which is the numbers at work.

34 Holmer, *The Paul L. Holmer Papers: On Kierkegaard and the Truth*, 216.

35 Ludwig Wittgenstein, *Philosophical Investigations*, trans. G.E.M. Anscombe (Oxford: Basil Blackwell, 1988), 224.

36 Holmer, *C.S. Lewis*, 29.

37 Ibid., 43.

38 Holmer, *The Paul L. Holmer Papers: On Kierkegaard and the Truth*, 36.

39 Holmer, *C.S. Lewis*, 65.

40 Holmer, *The Paul L. Holmer Papers: On Kierkegaard and the Truth*, 179–80.

41 Ibid., 122.

42 Holmer, *C.S. Lewis*, 65.

43 Holmer, *The Paul L. Holmer Papers: On Kierkegaard and the Truth*, 190.

44 Holmer, *C.S. Lewis*, 7.

45 Ibid., 86.

46 Ibid., 57.

47 Ibid., 93.

48 Holmer, *The Paul L. Holmer Papers: Thinking the Faith with Passion*, 209.

49 Holmer, *C.S. Lewis*, 23.

50 Holmer, *The Paul L. Holmer Papers: Thinking the Faith with Passion*, 46.

51 Holmer, *The Paul L. Holmer Papers: On Kierkegaard and the Truth*, 70.

52 Ibid., 56.

53 Ibid., 63.

54 Ibid., 61–2.

55 Ibid. 69.

56 Holmer, *The Paul L. Holmer Papers: Thinking the Faith with Passion*, 43–4.

57 Holmer, *The Paul L. Holmer Papers: On Kierkegaard and the Truth*, 63.

58 Holmer, *The Paul L. Holmer Papers: Thinking the Faith with Passion*, 210.

59 Hermann Sasse, "Scripture and the Church: Selected Essays of Hermann Sasse," *Concordia Seminary Monograph Series*, no. 2, ed. Jeffrey J. Kloha and Ronald R. Feuerhahn (Chelsea, MI: BookCrafters, 1995), 102. Note that Sasse is a conservative theologian of the Lutheran Church, and certainly not a "liberal" theologian.

60 Holmer, *The Paul L. Holmer Papers: Thinking the Faith with Passion*, 226.

61 Holmer, *The Paul L. Holmer Papers: Communicating the Faith Indirectly*, 14.

62 Holmer, *The Paul L. Holmer Papers: Thinking the Faith with Passion*, 212.

63 Ibid., 50.

64 Holmer, *The Paul L. Holmer Papers: Communicating the Faith Indirectly*, 83.

65 Holmer, *The Paul L. Holmer Papers: On Kierkegaard and the Truth*, 60–1.

66 Holmer, *C.S. Lewis*, 50–1.

67 Holmer, *The Paul L. Holmer Papers: Communicating the Faith Indirectly*, 47.

68 Ibid., 87.

69 Lewis, C. S., *The Screwtape Letters* (New York: Harper, 2001), Ch. 25.

70 Holmer, *The Paul L. Holmer Papers: Thinking the Faith with Passion*, 191.

71 Holmer, *The Paul L. Holmer Papers: On Kierkegaard and the Truth*, 57.

72 Ibid., 52.

73 Holmer, *The Paul L. Holmer Papers: Thinking the Faith with Passion*, 214.

2
Theology *Must* Be Projected

Brad J. Kallenberg

Paul Holmer writes at the intersection of two of the deepest and most provocative thinkers in the last two centuries: Søren Kierkegaard and Ludwig Wittgenstein. Although I cannot entirely prise these voices apart in Holmer's thought, the focus in the present essay is Holmer's absorption of Wittgenstein. Rather than draw upon essays in which he explicitly quotes Wittgenstein, I aim to show how thoroughly Holmer presumes Wittgenstein in his theology and writes in ways that display Wittgenstein's own method. My task is made more difficult by the scope and complexity of Wittgenstein's own vision. In addition, some of Holmer's expressions sound so obviously Kierkegaardian that one may easily miss the Wittgensteinian dialect in which they are cast. Nevertheless, there are some tells that tip off alert readers to just how many Wittgensteinian cards Holmer holds in his hand. To be specific, I will claim that when Holmer writes "theology has to be projected," he is envisioning what I will show to be projection in the Wittgensteinian sense.[1] I begin with a sketch of the problem and then proceed to introduce familiar Wittgensteinian themes en route to highlighting in Holmer the more obscure Wittgensteinian material upon which Holmer relies.

Holmer wrote in an age dominated by a kind of realism for which "truth" was taken to be a matter of (straightforward?) correspondence between a proposition and some state of affairs. But Holmer dissents, averring that within both religion and ethics a given sentence is not exhausted by its correspondence to reality. Swimming against the tide, he argues:

> The sentence also becomes something to actualize, and increasingly the attention is drawn from the relation between the sentence and objective states of affairs to the relation between the sentence as a proposal for one's life and one's life. This difference is not, of course, to be marked in the sentence as much as it is in the *use* of the sentence. This kind of sentence is not indifferent as to how the individual receives it.[2]

Without denying that there is such a thing as truth-as-objectivity, Holmer affirms Kierkegaard's insight that there is just as surely truth-as-subjectivity. Christian apologists argue that the sentence "Jesus is Lord" has objective truth value. But to say the same string of words and by it mean "Jesus is *my* Lord" is to take a stance regarding its truth-as-subjectivity. Perhaps not every reader of Kierkegaard perceives the significance and depth of this idea. But Holmer had decided that one person who read Kierkegaard in the proper spirit was Wittgenstein.

Wittgenstein's introduction to American scholarship on Kierkegaard was helped by a man from Kansas named Norman Malcolm. Malcolm attended Wittgenstein's lectures at Cambridge in 1939 and eventually joined the philosophy faculty at Cornell University.[3] Wittgenstein and Malcolm kept up regular correspondence. Wittgenstein once wrote to Malcolm that he found Kierkegaard's *Concluding Unscientific Postscript* "too deep," by which he meant not that Kierkegaard was difficult, but that he, Wittgenstein, was too shallow. "Kierkegaard is far too deep for me, anyhow," wrote Wittgenstein. "He bewilders me without working the good effects which he would in *deeper* souls."[4] In the same letter, Wittgenstein admitted to Malcolm that he'd not yet read Kierkegaard's *Works of Love*.[5] On Malcolm's recommendation, he agreed to do so and sought help in acquiring David and Lillian Swenson's then new English translation in preparation for publication by University of Princeton Press. Malcolm prevailed upon Paul Holmer at Yale, a friend of the Swenson, for a copy, which was then sent on to Wittgenstein. Eventually Malcolm reported back to Holmer: "Wittgenstein had already read [*Works of Love*] in the German translation, didn't like the German, had tried it in Danish and, because of his knowledge of Norwegian, he was able to read it; but it wasn't clear to him. So he wanted to try it in English translation." Despite the Swenson's excellent translation, Wittgenstein still found the writing "too high." When Holmer inquired what Wittgenstein meant by *that*, Malcolm wrote back: "It was as if he [Wittgenstein] couldn't manage those intense passions and feelings that were involved in Kierkegaard's volume." Holmer recalled further, "Malcolm pointed out to me that the lovely thing about Wittgenstein was that he didn't blame Kierkegaard for that. He thought it was his own weakness."[6] This reply made a deep impression on Holmer.

Wittgenstein's approach to understanding Christianity, like his reading of Kierkegaard, always began with the expectation that one would need first to "work on oneself."[7] Wittgenstein's attempt to read Kierkegaard in the proper spirit came to a head in his 1936–7 sabbatical. Wittgenstein secluded himself in a rural hut in Norway. (During some seasons, fetching supplies required rowing a small boat across a fjord.[8]) In recently translated diaries—some of which entries are so private that he wrote them in code—Wittgenstein makes it evident that his reading of Kierkegaard during his Norwegian exile was accompanied by active praying, and intensive Scripture reading culminating in public confessions of sin to a dozen or more people.[9] Although it is unclear whether Holmer himself read the so-called Koder diaries (known otherwise as MS 183), he clearly approved of what he saw in Wittgenstein's approach to thinking theologically.

One of the natural ways that Holmer described the relationship between Scripture and reader, between canon and congregation, was by employing the word "projection." Before unpacking this significance of this technical term, I must first clarify for unfamiliar readers the kind of Wittgensteinian landscape Holmer presumes. I will sketch this quickly and in four broad strokes. I will not defend Wittgenstein's thought; my goal is simply to bring into the foreground the Wittgensteinian background to Holmer's thought.

1. Language constitutes[10] the world

Which of the following maxims is to be preferred?

- "In the beginning was the Word" [Luther's Bible "*Im Anfang war das Wort*"[11]]
- "In the beginning is the relation" [Martin Buber, *Im Anfang ist die Beziehung.*[12]]
- "In the beginning was the deed" [Goethe, *Im Anfang war die Tat*[13]]

Holmer learned from Wittgenstein to affirm all three. By the power of the word, God spoke the universe into being (Ps 31:9). As creatures made in the image of the divine, human beings also speak words that bring "worlds" into being: a verbally abusive parent creates the twisted reality that the abused child inhabits. Wittgenstein would have also approved Buber's qualification of "in the beginning" (Gen. 1:1) to emphasis the priority of relation because sentences do not hang in a void. Rather, each sentence presupposes a speaker (I) and a hearer (Thou) who stand in some kind of relation prior to, or constituted by, the speaking.[14] And Wittgenstein explicitly affirmed Goethe's dictum because *words do stuff*. Words are rarely simply pictures of states of affairs as in the sophomore philosophy example, "The cat is on the mat." When *promising, asking, cursing, thanking, praying,* and so on, our words are doing work.[15] Depicting may be *a* function, but it is not *the sole* function of language. Picturing takes its place in a line of myriads upon myriads of actions that words can perform. If anything, words are more akin to *tools* than to pictures.[16] Words are better understood as performative rather than depictive. Picturing is not excluded as a function of language, just prevented from being the primary, much less the only, function of language.[17]

If "picturing" is partly correct (or correct some of the time) as a model of how language works, why does Wittgenstein make such a fuss in order to loosen the grip of this model on our imagination? The answer lies in the fact that the Western philosophers have been inordinately insistent upon the totalizing scope of the picture theory of language—that language fundamentally depicts to us states of affairs. This bad habit is at least as old as Descartes and was perpetuated in turn by John Locke, David Hume, Immanuel Kant, straight on through to Wittgenstein's one-time teacher, Bertrand Russell. The picture theory turns upon the trenchant assumption that language is one thing and the world (or "Reality") is *something else*, in particular, a vast composite of *non*linguistic "states of affairs." On this model, the true sentence, or more precisely "proposition," is the verbal picture that corresponds to the respective state of affairs. And "correspondence" was typically thought to be assessable with reference to empirical evidence. In other words, one can look and see that the cat is on the mat, so the sentence "The cat is on the mat" is therefore true!

Herein lies a problem: if language is externally related to the world, one can never achieve absolute certainty. One might get pretty close to certainty, but never 100 percent. (Only in syllogisms of symbolic logic and mathematical calculations might certainty be attained.) So Russell writes:

> It *seems* to me that I am now sitting in a chair, at a table of a certain shape, on which I see sheets of paper with writing or print.... I *believe* that, if any other normal person comes into my room, he will see the same chairs and tables and books and papers that I see, and that the table which I see is the same as the table which I feel pressing against my arm. All this

seems to be so evident as to be hardly worth stating, except in answer to a man who doubts whether I know anything. *Yet all this may be reasonably doubted ....*[18]

In the empiricist outlook expressed by Russell, the best one could do to establish the truthfulness of a sentence was to verify it by sensory data. The more points of data there are, the better. The better the sensory faculties reporting the data are, the better. But 100 percent certainty is never quite arrived at because it is excluded by the logical possibility of doubt. "Yet all this may be reasonably doubted."

Wittgenstein asks us to reconsider whether the time-honored position of skepticism squares with human experience. A philosophical skeptic may stand outside in a downpour, shivering and spluttering, and ask, "I *seem* to be wet. I *believe* I am wet. But how do I *know* that I am wet? All this can reasonably be doubted." The dripping philosopher presumes the key issue at hand is "know"—"How do I *know* that I am wet?" But Wittgenstein observes that the philosopher unwittingly acts with *absolute* certainty. How so? Because the philosopher has employed the correct word for the occasion: *wet*. The philosopher doesn't ask "How do I know that I'm accelerating?" Or " ... cowardly?" Or " ... short?" Or " ... Spanish?" In reflexively using the word "wet" the philosopher gives the game away. Perhaps there is certainty after all.

The crucial conclusion, on Wittgenstein's understanding, and thus for Holmer as well, is that language doesn't *correspond* to the world, rather language *constitutes* the world. Language and world are internally related. And that is something that cannot be diagrammed.

This conclusion is not to say Wittgenstein was some sort of "non-realist" or "anti-realist."[19] Realism is fine as far as it goes. It is the bifurcation of language from world that is unthinkable: "Not empiricism and yet realism in philosophy, that is the hardest thing."[20] Language is never one thing and the world another. (Nor, importantly, does language reduce to words.) Human beings perceive the world by means of fluency in language. Wittgenstein asks, "How do I know that this color is red?—It would be an answer to say 'I have learnt English.'"[21] The "world" is not merely bare rocks, trees, and other middle-sized dry goods. If we are honest with ourselves, our world also includes social relationships, structures of power, the economy, the law, history, etc. All of these we have access to by means of language.[22]

2. Grammar entails certainty

Of equal importance to the notion that language constitutes the world, that the boundary of one's "reality" is coterminous with one's fluency in a conceptual language, is the realization that for Wittgenstein, "language" does not reduce to brute "words." We communicate with each other by all sort of means—facial expressions, body language, tone of voice (e.g., sarcasm), sketches on the backs of envelopes, even gestures. Norman Malcolm reported on conversations Wittgenstein held with Italian economist Piero Sraffa.

> Wittgenstein was insisting that a proposition and that which it describes must have the same "logical form," [or "grammar" depending on which version of the story is quoted] the same "logical multiplicity," Sraffa made a gesture, familiar to Neapolitans as meaning something like disgust or contempt, of brushing the underneath of his chin with an outward sweep of the finger-tips of one hand. And he asked: "What is the logical form of *that*?"[23]

While the story may be apocryphal, the point is made poignantly: gestures and words are reciprocally related.

> How curious: we should like to explain our understanding of a gesture by means of translation into words, and the understanding of words by translating them into a gesture. (Thus we are tossed to and fro when we try to find out where understanding properly resides.)[24]

This is not to say that gestures ought to be treated as wordless words. (If that were so, then gestures would pose the same problem as words, namely, where does meaning reside?) Rather, meaning gets its life from the interplay of body movements and vocalization. But the list can't stop at only two items, gestures and words. Wittgenstein would later write that "gestures no less than words are intertwined in a *net of multifarious relationships*."[25] To the interplay of gestures and words must be added things like particular context, the skills and biography of the speakers, the cultural habits and even the history of the community.

Language is indeed rule-governed. But the rules of grammar do not govern from above, but are read off the play of the game "from within," as it were. Wittgenstein instructs his students: "It is part of the grammar of the word 'chair' that this [said while proceeding to sit down] is what we call 'to sit on a chair' …."[26] Wittgenstein is implying that we in the West have a deeper fluency with chairs than might an aboriginal people who comfortably squat on their haunches. One might succeed in teaching the "aboriginal" group to pick out chairs from a line-up of objects. But if the word "chair" is simply learned as a label, then the learners will have trouble distinguishing chairs from tables, not to mention stools. Their difficulty in really understanding the concept of *chair* will persist until they participate in our grammar, when they, like us, begin to sit *on* chairs and sit *at* tables. For Wittgenstein, the bodily and social activities associated with a given concept he calls the "grammar" of the concept. Note: "grammar" does not refer to a list of rules gathered into a book. Rather for Wittgenstein, grammar indicates regular and shared ways of acting in which a given word is "at home."[27] The act of sitting doesn't exhaust the grammar of "chair." Becoming fluent in the grammar of "chair" also includes counting chairs as well as fetching, stacking, re-upholstering, losing pocket change into, rearranging, hiding behind, pulling up, stubbing toes on, and so on.

Grammatical fluency is where certainty resides. The certainty that accompanies language use is not bound up with the amassing of sensory data, the calculating of probabilities, and the drawing of inferences as might be the case for the philosopher or the scientist who seek justification for claims and hypotheses. For both the philosopher and the scientist, the greater the quantity and quality of data, the greater ought one's degree of confidence be. The philosopher W.K. Clifford famously said in 1877, "It is wrong always, everywhere, and for anyone, to believe anything upon insufficient evidence."[28] One hundred and forty years later, Neil deGrasse Tyson said much the same thing when asked "What do you need to believe in order to get through the day?" He answered, "Assuming you mean belief without evidence, there is no such thing in my life."[29] Yet evidentialism turns out *not* to be the functional baseline of our day-to-day existence. When we utilize language, we most often react instantly and without weighing evidence. A child skins her knee and instantly cries. An adult who skins her knee will reflexively cry out, perhaps saying "Ouch!" instead of crying. Here the word "ouch!" goes proxy for crying. (It could go either way.) In both cases, the reactions are neither of inference nor of choice. There is simply reaction. She may say "Ouch!" or "Wow—that really smarts!" or say nothing at all. (Of course, it is equally important that at the moment of injury the victim does not blurt out "The cat is on the mat.") And those nearby immediately understand their cries and sympathize. Both victim and sympathizer instinctively rely on language to do its job.

Of course, our dispositions to act (or react) one way rather than others can be inappropriate or even deceptive. And our fluencies can be formed (or deformed) by slow training over time. Moreover, there are times when it *is* best to hold one's tongue so as to reflect before speaking. All this is granted. But these are special cases within the overall condition of linguistic certainty and interpersonal trust. The kind of instinctive certainty involved in the giving of linguistic responses is nothing like the probability calculated by cool-headed inference. Wittgenstein called this categorical difference the difference between *criterial* and *symptomatic* thinking.

Allow me to recall the drenched philosopher standing out in the rain. The philosophical skeptic treats his statement ("I believe it to be the case that I am wet") as an empirical claim, one that stands in need of testing and verification. But, strictly speaking, testing is premature. In assessing the claim, "It is the case that X," one must first know *what* "X" means before one can begin to consider *whether* X is (or is not) the case. These are two separate issues. To borrow an early example from Wittgenstein, imagine the claim, "Bismarck's toothache is getting worse." *What* the sense of "toothache" amounts to cannot be settled by enumerating symptoms. It has to be settled by something prior to and *more basic* than symptoms (or else the discussion can never begin). The sense of the term "toothache" is bound up with holding one's jaw, mumbling, moaning, insomnia, and so on. As sitting is to the concept of *chair*, holding one's jaw is part of the *grammar* of *toothache*. The point is not that toothache *causes* Bismarck to hold his jaw but rather, holding one's jaw is partly constitutive of the sense of the concept "toothache." All such things fall under the conceptual umbrella of *criteria*.[30]

By contrast, *symptoms* enter the conversation subsequently, logically later, after we have reflexively employed criteria in our knowing *what* is being talking about. Bismarck does not have a flat tire, an overdrawn bank account or a wife who beats him. He has a toothache. Once this much is clear, we can decide if Bismarck's toothache is worsening.

Wittgenstein only bothers to mention the symptomatic mode of reasoning once in the entire *Investigations*, and then only to contrast it with the criterial mode.

The fluctuation in grammar between criteria and symptoms makes it look as if there were nothing at all but symptoms. We say, for example: "Experience teaches that there is rain when the barometer falls, but it also teaches that there is rain when we have certain sensations of wet and cold, or such-and-such visual impressions."

Inferring rain from a falling barometer is *symptomatic* reasoning. Seeing raindrops fall and sensing wet and cold on the skin comprise the *criterial*, because these bodily experiences, which are recognizable from past experiences, are parts of the grammar of "rain."

Wittgenstein happily concedes that sense-impressions may deceive us. However, he goes on to say, what we are *not* deceived about is that we call this "rain." Wittgenstein continues, "The point here is not that our sense-impressions might lie, but that we understand their language." Moreover, "this language like any other is founded on convention."[31] The drenched philosopher reacts with absolute certainty by using the word "wet" (*criterially*) in order to express doubt about a *symptomatically* fashioned conclusion: "How do I know I'm wet?" The language games involving the word "rain" are founded on the long-standing convention that we each and all share reactions such as "Hey! (looking up–blink! blink!) It's *raining*!"

In order for symptomatic, or inferential, reasoning to function, a whole language must already be in place.[32] Not just in place for this individual, but for a whole community of speakers. Each individual is trained into a language that has been already in play long before he or she is born. The philosopher reacts with unthinking certainty in using the word "wet"; no inference, no calculation, no induction—pure grammatical certainty.

To the points that (1) language constitutes a world and (2) grammar entails certainty, a third emerges.

3. Theology coaches for grammatical fluency in a world-constituting language

Wittgenstein has only one thing to say about theology in the *Investigations* and this is the mysterious parenthetical aphorism: "(Theology as grammar)."[33] In the immediate context, Wittgenstein is contrasting "grammar" with the empiricist's urge to settle every question either by *pointing* to the thing itself (ostensive definition) or pointing to the evidence for the thing (evidentialism).[34] But Wittgenstein observed that pointing settles nothing.

> Point to a piece of paper—And now point to its shape—now to its colour—now to its number (that sounds queer)—How did you do it?—You will say that you "meant" a different thing

each time you pointed. And if I ask how that is done, you will say you concentrated your attention on the colour, the shape, etc. But I ask again: how is that done?[35]

Even the simple gesture of pointing requires a huge array of shared concepts, reactions, and behaviors to be in place; to repeat: gestures and words are interdependent. (Indonesian inhabitants of Iran Jaya point not with their index finger but *with their lips*.)

As a replacement for the inferior ostensive definition, Wittgenstein offers "grammatical investigation"—because the criterial question ("*What* is *X*?") is answered by observing its grammar, that is, *how the concept is used* in communication in concrete situations. The activity of weighing belongs to the concept of *cheese* but not to the concept of *cloud* because we actually weigh blocks of cheese at the grocers, but no one can imagine weighing a cloud. If a block of cheese expanded or contracted randomly (as a cloud does) then we wouldn't talk of the weight of cheese.[36] How we actually speak about cheese and clouds displays what sort of reality blocks of cheese and clouds are. Similarly for theology. Theology is not a giant system of verified propositions. Rather, theology for Wittgenstein, as for Holmer in Wittgenstein's wake, involves developing fluency regarding how religious believers live with words like "Jesus," "God," "sin," "redemption," and "love." Their use of such words embodies and displays what kind of reality these concepts connote. And not only these special words, but words about "everything else as well."³⁷ And now I'll begin bringing Paul Holmer more directly into the mix.

> For theology does not parse verbs, arrange thoughts, and conjugate sentences. Its matter is finally the whole of human life itself. Insofar as it is a grammar, it is more like the teaching that leads to a truly successful, deeply satisfactory, even blessed and happy life.³⁸

Theology is totalizing. Theology has to do with everything, just like language.

Born into a social world, human beings navigate by moving in a largely predictable pattern of acting, reacting, and judging that keeps to a minimum surprises between family and neighbors. This regularity is not chosen nor voted upon. It just is. And we all participate. We all squint at bright lights and brake at red lights. These deeply habitual reactions are thoroughly automatic and entirely non-inferential. Even our thought processes follow familiar and automatic tracks:

> [T]he rules of reasoning are the *criteria* [of our thinking]; but the rules of reasoning are finally a part of the very grammar of how we are living, behaving, wanting, and judging. The *criteria* become manifest in the way we live.³⁹

For Holmer as well as Wittgenstein, criterial certainty lies at the bottom of being human.

> It is what human beings say that is true and false; and they agree in the language they use. That is not agreement in opinions but in form of life. If language is to be a means of communication there must be agreement not only in definitions but also (queer as this may sound) in judgments.[40]

If a long string laying on the floor outside my office suddenly begins to slide past my door, I do not wonder "Who is *pushing* that string?" The fact that we all unthinkingly concur in our reactions is embedded in the shape of our automatic question: "Who is *pulling* that string?" That's what my grandchildren call "a no-brainer." All who share "no-brainer" reactions share a world. We cannot simply get together and vote to share different no-brainer reactions. (We cannot simply choose to seek out pushers of string.) And the lone-ranger who opts out of our deep conventions cannot but run into trouble. Wittgenstein:

> [T]hinking and inferring (like counting) is of course bounded for us, not by an arbitrary definition, but by natural limits corresponding to the body of what can be called the role of thinking and inferring in our life.

For we are at one over this, that the laws of inference do not compel him to say or to write such and such like rails compelling a locomotive....nevertheless the laws of inference can be said to compel us; in the same sense, that is to say, as other laws in human society. [A worker] would be punished if he inferred differently. *If you draw different conclusions you do indeed get into conflict, e.g. with society; and also with other practical consequences.*[41]

One cannot simply make a new conceptual world by wishing it to be so. However, one may be *converted* to a new world.

Wittgensteinians like Holmer say that those who operate by the same deep criteria share a "world." However, Holmer goes beyond some Wittgensteinians by insisting that there are two worlds to consider: the natural social world into which one is born and the religious world into which one may be "converted."[42]

Holmer understands the scope of "theology" to be as extensive as St. Paul understands conversion. While our highly individualized culture often leads us to read passages in the New Testament in narrow ways, a close study of Paul's Corinthian correspondence explains that to be "in Christ"—a phrase used more than twenty times in just the Corinthian epistles—means entering into a whole "new world."[43] Everything is new. It is not a case of simply "I'm a new creature." That is too small. Rendered literally, St. Paul says "If anyone is in Christ, new world!" Here

St. Paul contrasts the "new" reality with the "old" world, the fallen and enslaved creation, the everyday social reality of great evils but also of ordinary struggles and ordinary language.

When Saul was converted, he was blind for three days, before being renamed "Paul."[44] In a crucial sense, he never saw the old world again. For when his sight was miraculously restored, it was *kainē ktisis*—a whole new world, one in which nothing was seen in the former manner. Thereafter, even human persons were no longer recognized according to physical features (i.e., "according to the flesh").[45]

In Christian conversion, the believer becomes a baby as it were, a child who will learn to inhabit a world by gaining fluency in all the necessary concepts.[46] A human child must learn the words "string," "cheese," and "string cheese." So too, the neophyte believer must absorb the grammar of "love," "justice," and "mercy." Holmer notes:

> We can learn grammar and logic as a separate set of rules, or we can sometimes learn to speak logically and grammatically *simply by conforming to the practice of those who know how.* In either case, the closer we come to successful practice ourselves, the less overt our knowledge of the rules and the more tacit and informing those rules actually become. We finally become grammatical and logical in all that we say, even if we are hard put to state any longer the rules themselves ....

> Theology ... must be absorbed, and when it is, the hearer is supposed to become Godly.[47]

So while theology concerns the grammar of this new conceptual language, theologians are *not*, as commonly supposed, the builders of abstruse and complex systems. On Holmer's view, the point is to "become grammatical in speaking about everything."[48] Just as a child learning a first language absorbs its grammar, so too the adolescent Christian matures—becomes Godly—by absorbing the grammar called theology. In some instances, learning the "rules" may be helpful. But the "rules" are not set in stone, nor do they exist apart from the living of this language in community. Theology is forever in flux, always "dependent upon a consensus of belief and practices" displayed both by Jesus (together with his earliest followers) and by contemporary "lives limned by [Scripture's] pages."[49]

Would-be learners of the Christian conceptual language face an ongoing challenge: because the patterns of our speaking are not permanently fixed, fluency is never mastered once and for all.

> Though we can learn about God from the Bible, we are also expected to *become* learners, to learn as we go, from living in accord with Jesus, and with Apostolic faithfulness in mind. Our walking by faith is also an *ongoing learning* about God.[50]

Holmer states the task in starkest terms: how do we live the language called "Christian" in keeping with its Spirit? "[I]f theology is grammar, then there is the task, always pertinent, of learning to *extend* the rules, the order, the morphology, of Godliness over the ever-changing circumstances."[51] What might this extension entail?

4. Fluency entails "projection"

When the notion of "projection" is used with respect to language, the typical default position is to imagine "projection" as something like "translation." For example, we assume "Pepper is black" can be projected into German by the sentence, "Pfeffer ist Schwarz." Here we see a straight one-to-one mapping of words: Pepper becomes "Pfeffer," "is" becomes "ist," and "black" is rendered as "Schwartz." While word-for-word same-saying works in some cases, it cannot be taken as epitomizing how "projection" works. To the extent we confuse word-swapping for projection, we'd miss what Holmer was trying to accomplish.

Holmer employs the term "projection" a surprising number of times, tying it specifically to the Christian theological task: "I say again that theology has to be *projected*."[52]

The whole business of using theology as grammar requires also that we refer our nation, our world, our selves, our future to God. These very terms are dramatic and sweeping. It takes imagination to use them. It is as if the whole of life were God's theatre—we are all actors and God is the only spectator. Within that kind of *projection*, that imaginative construct, we begin to get the hang of ourselves and the world. We move, then, from saying with Paul that he lives no longer "I," that Christ lives in him, to start to live that way ourselves. This is where the positive *projection* of real preaching becomes theology in action. It works as it envelopes the hearer in the divine correction of disposition, or love, or orientation that is life-long.[53]

In this single paragraph, Holmer unites Kierkegaard to Wittgenstein. In 1847, Kierkegaard argued that in the theater of life, God is the audience and we—ordinary believers, that is, rather than the paid professionals—are the performers.[54] Our presentation is not dull, wooden, lifeless chanting of a memorized script but something animated, new, *lived*. German readers will appreciate that for his part Wittgenstein placed much greater emphasis on *Darstellung* than on *Vorstellung*. Both German terms get translated as "(re)presentation" in English. One can "present" a film at a cinema (*vorstellen*) but in live theater, one must *re*-present (*darstellen*). A film is the same every time it is played. But live drama is never quite the same. Sometimes it is slightly different, and other times it may even be vastly different, depending on context. (Even though Wittgenstein delivered lectures in English, Wittgenstein couldn't bear any lack of clarity that English entailed. On at least one occasion he reverted to the German word *Darstellung* so that attendees would not mistake his emphasis.[55])

The activity of projection [*Projektion*], the wide variety of *methods* of projection [*Projektionsmethode*] and the resulting prototype or representation [*Darstellung*] were technical concepts Wittgenstein retained from his engineering education long after he had retired his slide rule.[56] In this section, I will show what work these engineering concepts perform for Wittgenstein en route to showing how the terms shed light on Holmer's theological project.

In 1939, Wittgenstein delivered a set of lectures on the foundations of mathematics the students' notes of which were later published. In these lectures he is quoted as explaining:

> For there may be many different techniques of comparison and many different kinds of resemblance. For instance, one thing may be said to resemble another if it is a projection of it; but there are *many different modes of projection*—of representing an object.[57]

He is not speaking of representing an object to oneself but to others, in an act of communication. To novice engineering students, "method of projection" would have triggered images of technical drawings such as Figure 1.

The pyramid is projected onto three planes by means of rays that intersect each plane at 90° (thus this method is called "othogonal projection"). If the object being projected is complicated, students can be tested on their ability to "read" the projections and decide whether the projected views are correct or incorrect. Engineering students facing such an exam question know that there is an objective answer, because the method of projection is precise and can be completely spelled out in advance. For example, none of the side views of this

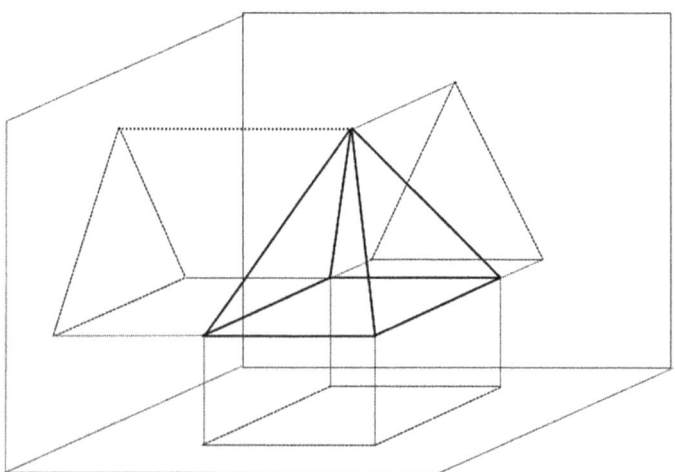

FIGURE 1 *Orthogonal Projection.*

pyramid are circles! (This is the basis of Computer Aided Design; the entire process can be performed by a computer; no human needed.) But the question of correctness quickly becomes trickier if the *Projektionsmethode* itself is altered. The desk at which I sit looks trapezoidal to me because I'm viewing it at an angle other than 90º.

A coin as it spins is experienced by viewers as variously elliptical as it rotates through angles to the viewer other than 90º. Wittgenstein offered even strangers forms of projection. On one occasion, Wittgenstein even asked his students to envision a square projected onto a *circle*. (One might imagine a sculptor fashioning a vase with a square base but a circular top.) Here the *Projektionsmethode* is not simply non-orthogonal. It is an entirely different breed, and seemingly impossible to spell out mathematically.[58] If a square in Plane I can be projected onto a circle in Plane II, why not triangles and trapezoids? Of course, that *is* possible too. And in such mappings, viewing one of the circles in Plane II apparently tells the viewer nothing whatsoever about the original shape in Plane I. For each shape in Plane I, a

FIGURE 2 *Oblique projection.*

distinct *Projektionsmethode* would be needed—one for squares, another for triangles, another for trapezoids, and so on. Only if one had mastered all the skills of the relevant *Projektionsmethoden* could one move accurately between Planes I and II (from circle to square or circle to trapezoid, or whatever).

By these somewhat bizarre examples, Wittgenstein is trying to draw attention to the sheer variety of *skill sets* needed for performing such sui generis projections. For Wittgenstein, language use, like technical drawing in engineering, involves projection. The mastery needed by each of us to navigate the linguistic world may be rendered transparent to the extent we mistakenly think language is nothing but a concatenation of word-pictures. But if we consider carefully, even in the simplest of cases (namely, describing an object), our employment of language is not a mere snapshot, but itself a skillful projection.

> What we call "descriptions" [*Beschreibungen*] are instruments for particular uses. Think of a machine-drawing, a cross-section, an elevation with measurements, which an engineer has before him. Thinking of a description as a word-picture of the facts has something misleading about it: one tends to think only of such pictures as hang on our walls: which seem simply to portray how a thing looks, what it is like.[59]

To repeat his warning: "Thinking of a description as a word-picture of the facts has something misleading about it." One cannot find the grocery store by using an orienteering map any more than one can estimate a watershed by using a road map. Nor can one drive to Kansas City from New York by using cartoonist Saul Steinberg's "View of the World from 9th Avenue."[60] In point of fact, every attempt at projecting some section of the globe called "earth" onto two dimensions inevitably entails distortion. Some deviations from the facts are intentional, as when subway maps are drastically simplified for usability.[61] Granted, the demand for skill on the side of the artist (the "projectionist" as it were) may be greater than the skills required by viewers. But sometimes great skill is required on both sides. For example, a surgeon must recognize an infected mass, grossly inflamed to many times its healthy size, as a projection of what is recalled as the tidy diagram of a gall bladder memorized from the med school textbook. If the surgeon cannot perform this projection, he or she will be unable to diagnose and correct the problem.[62]

Wittgenstein thought that even a smiley face could be taken as a projection of a famous face, say that of fellow Cambridge don, G.E. Moore:

Suppose I said, "This [smiley face] is a picture of Moore. It's an exact picture, but in a new projection …."-If I say, "This is a picture of him", it immediately suggests a certain way of usage. For instance, I might say, "Go and meet So-and-so at the station; you will know him because this [photo] is a picture of him." Then you may take the picture and use it to find him. But you couldn't do the same with my [cartoon] picture of Moore. You don't understand my picture of Moore because *you don't know how* to use it.[63]

In this discussion, Wittgenstein is trying to cut short the objection that the smiley face is a *bad* picture of Moore. No, he says, it is *exact*. But we as viewers can agree to its exactitude if and only if we *know how to use* the picture (e.g., to pick Moore out of a crowd at the station). If it can be done, it will only be because the liaison (who hasn't met Moore) has mastered the *Projektionsmethode*. In this case, *the onus is on the viewer to possess skills adequate* for reading the projection, that is, to work in reverse from the smiley face to picking out the right stranger (i.e., Moore) from a crowd. An even more poignant example is posed by Wittgenstein in a later discussion.

Suppose an art teacher, beginning with a poster depicting a unicorn—of the sort admired by my granddaughter—demonstrates to the class a step-by-step process for drawing a reasonable facsimile. Having done so, the artist has herself projected the original object (unicorn) onto a surface. Then the art teacher turns to the class: "Now you do the same." Each student, at whatever level of skill, knows precisely what is expected: to

THEOLOGY *MUST* BE PROJECTED 67

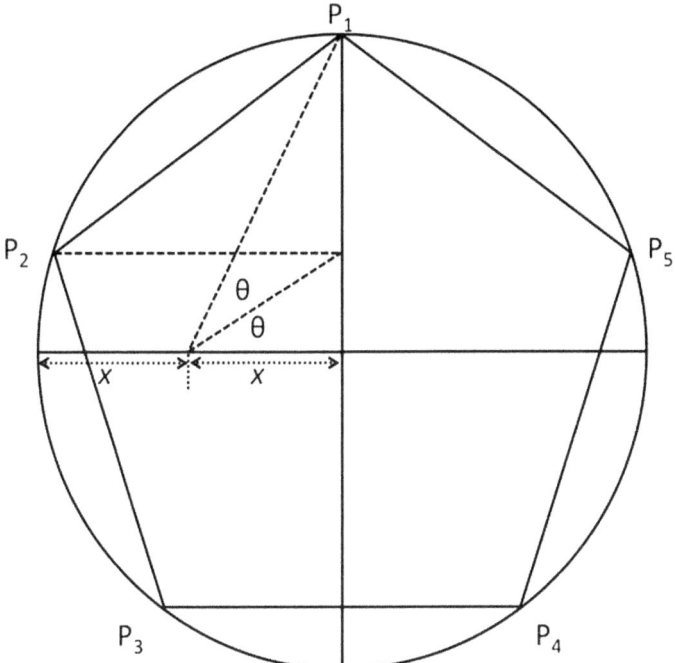

FIGURE 3 *Inscribed Pentagon.*

copy the unicorn poster. So far, so good. Wittgenstein morphs the illustration for the sake of pedagogy. Suppose next, Wittgenstein continues, a geometry teacher shows students how to inscribe a pentagon inside a circle using a compass and straight edge.[64]

No doubt geometry students could deduce the recipe from the diagram and go on to inscribe their own pentagon. Then the teacher throws a curve ball, "Now you do the analogous thing for a heptadecagon (a 17-sided polygon)!" What is being requested is still a two-dimensional picture. However, the case is *entirely different*.[65] In the case of the unicorn, the "method of projection" is easily apprehended, even if much practice is needed to master the execution. Whether the object is a unicorn, a bowl of fruit, or pastoral landscape, the method of projection is unchanged. But in this second case, the geometry students cannot even begin to imagine the *Projektionsmethode*. Clearly, they have no trouble envisioning the final product—a regular polygon with seventeen sides. But they cannot imagine how to get there. (Nor does their problem lie in the fact that the task is impossible. It is not; geometric methods for inscribing a 17-gon have been devised.[66])

In the case of the unicorn, what is being requested is a reapplication of a familiar method of projection. We might call the art students' task a form of "translation." In translation, students are expected to project an *object*. They can check their execution as they proceed by comparing the projection (their drawing) with the original (the unicorn poster). In the second case, what is projected is not an object. Rather, what is projected is a *method* of projection. (We might call this second-order projection a case of *meta-projection*.) Clearly *some* skill is required in the first case—especially hand-eye coordination—in order to project a recognizable unicorn onto one's own pad; perhaps some student renderings are ugly or barely recognizable. But it takes an altogether higher order of skill to project a *Projektionsmethode*. The math students are asked to project *Projektionsmethode*$_A$

(the recipe for inscribing a pentagon) onto *Projektionsmethode*$_B$ (some as yet unknown method of inscribing a 17-gon). The second method of projection is an utter transformation of the first method of projection despite the fact that both are comprised of the same basic geometric techniques (bisecting angles, constructing parallel lines, etc., using only a compass and ruler). This seems like an impossible task. But Holmer takes Wittgenstein to be saying meta-projection happens within language quite naturally and more often than we are likely to have noticed. In the next section, I'll describe linguistic meta-projection before going on to trace the way Holmer sees theology as meta-projection.

5. Linguistic fluency calls for meta-projection

Before the digital revolution, schoolchildren could make reasonable reproductions of, say, a unicorn poster by using a machine called the "opaque projector." Unlike the overhead models that used clear transparencies, the opaque projector enabled the student to place a picture under the hood and, if the lights were dimmed, the image would be (orthogonally) projected onto easel paper taped to the wall for convenient tracing. More advanced art students would be asked to project the image onto canvas without the aid of an opaque projector. In both instances, the assignment is a first-order projection, because the student has the advantage of comparing the projection with the original: Does my unicorn look like the original figure? Such is first-order projection. Holmer insisted that theology cannot simply be delivered (passively, like the mail), nor moved from "one mind to another in a direct and immediate way," nor can it simply be "translated" from one spatiotemporal context to another.[67] Holmer claims that theological interpretation is rarely a case of first-order projection, but rather *meta*-projection.

What makes theology a case of *meta*-projection is the fact that neither the object (i.e., religious concepts) nor the "method of projection" can be nailed down. *Both may change over time.* This ceaseless ambiguity belongs to the very nature of human communication. A smile in one context may be benevolent but, in another context, malicious. Surprisingly, we manage to communicate in spite of the ambiguity and flexibility. In some cases we can communicate precisely *because* the ambiguity is not ruled out. Wittgenstein scholar, Stanley Cavell, helps us see how.

Examples of linguistic meta-projection are plentiful but often missed because they are hidden in plain sight. Consider the innocuous verb "to feed." A child will pick up this concept while listening to mother, "Hold on a minute—I've got *to feed* your sister before we go to the park." Perhaps the child is given a daily chore. "This is how we *feed* the dog: take Marvin's bowl and …."

Eventually, mom and the child (with sister in tow), make it to the park where "*to feed* the ducks" is a fun activity. Cavell observes:

> We learn the use of "feed the kitty", "feed the lion", "feed the swans", and one day one of us says "feed the meter", or "feed in the film", or "feed the machine", or "feed his pride", or "feed wire", and we understand, we are not troubled.[68]

Cavell identifies two sorts of projections. That the first group—feed the kitty, the lion, the swans—are cases of first-order projection. Just as the teacher draws the unicorn and the students "do the same," so too the zookeeper puts Big-Cat food in the Big Kitty's bowl, and the child happily "does the same" by lobbing hunks of bread into the swan pond. By contrast, the latter group—feed the meter, feed in the film, feed his pride—seems to require a method of projection that is far trickier to specify (and in some cases cannot be specified at all). After all, coins are not food to the parking meter—the meter does not grow larger after "eating coins" nor will it wither and die without daily currency. Perhaps then we should conclude that "to feed" is a poor way to say it? Shouldn't we aspire to the plainest language possible to avoid misunderstanding?

Cavell wonders whether the unspecifiability of the method of projection tempts us to substitute a more general term. If we use "put" in the place of "feed," Cavell asks what, if anything, is gained? And more importantly, what is lost by insisting on disambiguation?

> What are our choices? We could use a more general verb, like "put", and say merely "Put the money in the meter", "Put new material into the machine", "Put film into the camera", etc. But first, that merely deprives us of a way of speaking which can discriminate differences which, in some instances, will be of importance; e.g., it does not discriminate between putting a flow of material into a machine and putting a part made of some new material into the construction of the machine. And it would begin to deprive us of the concept we have of the emotions. Is the idea of feeding pride or hope or anxiety any more metaphorical, any less essential to the concept of an emotion, than the idea that pride and hope, etc., grow and, moreover, grow on certain circumstances? Knowing what sorts of circumstances these are and what the consequences and marks of over-feeding are, is *part of knowing what pride is*.[69]

Cavell's analysis brings to light how deeply language is embedded in our living. There are no stand-alone linguistic "atoms" that have properties in isolation from context (as an atom has mass). If we imagine that "feeding the meter" is merely an ornamental metaphor, then it can be discarded for something more literal. But the fact is: any preference for a putative literal substitute, whether we are talking about parking meters or pride, *comes at the price of failing to understand ourselves.* The way we understand soulish terms such as "feelings of pride" is immediately attenuated if meta-projection is disallowed in favor of putative plain-speak. If pride is not the sort of thing that can be "fed" then it is not the sort of thing that "grows" on its own or "spreads like a weed." But are not these images (and others) *essential* to comprehending the evils of pride?

And really, Cavell presses us, is the supposedly more literal substitution of "put" any less complicated? Is the word "put" any less deeply ingressed in our lives? Does use of "put" require any less skill when it is projected into new contexts?

> For in order that "put" be a relevant candidate for this function, it must be the same word we use in contexts like "Put the cup on the saucer", "Put your hands over your head", "Put out the cat", "Put on your best armor", "Put on your best manner", "Put out the light and then put out the light."[70]

All concepts—whether "to feed" or "to put"—are deeply entangled with skillful ways of living. These skillful ways of living, which is to say skillful projections of concepts and of reading and responding to other's projections, are essential to human interacting and communicating, even when these skills cannot be definitively articulated but at most gestured at by a parade of examples.[71]

Because Holmer sees theology as a case of meta-projection, neither an exclusive focus on the object (religious stories, concepts, etc.) nor hopes placed upon detailing a straightforward method of projection will succeed. Rather, the way forward for theology is to take seriously the fact that we are creatures capable of developing tacit skills that contribute to the task of imaginatively projecting the Gospel into the twenty-first century.

6. Theology calls for (meta-)projection

In the essay "Kierkegaard and Christianity" Holmer grants that there is a cognitive component to Christianity. However, for Kierkegaard, faith itself is not mere cognitive "contemporaneity." In other words, to have faith does not mean adopting a stance in which *what* one believes lines up with *what* the apostles believed. If it were, then cognitive contemporaneity could be reduced to something like subscription to a standard set of doctrinal tenets. For Holmer, as for Kierkegaard, faith is not a *cognitive* contemporaneity but a *passionate* one.

Holmer follows Kierkegaard in understanding Christianity to be the alignment of one's passions with those exemplified in the New Testament church. To be a passionate contemporary means having the passions, desires, loves, wishes, joys, sorrows, hopes, gut reflexes (and so on) of a first-century believer. In order to become this, one must (a) *project* oneself back into the text of Scripture and (b) *project* the scriptural world forward into the present. Holmer describes the first projection this way.[72]

> But the active pedagogy in which [the teachings of the Bible] are exercised must insinuate the listener into a new role; his self-evaluation, his subjectivity, his aims, wishes, hopes, desires, must be altered so that the grammar of faith becomes relevant [to him]. When the right supposal envelopes him, when he understands himself to be a prisoner, a victim, a sinner, a changeling, then the teachings will come to life.[73]

Theology is therefore a life-giving experience: "This imaginative projection is the proper kind of popularization. It is popularization by vivification, not by vulgarization."[74] Theology doesn't strive to bring the Gospel down to the level of the hearer (whether by translation or paraphrase or some other strategy), but raises the hearer up to the level of the Gospel. This elevation doesn't happen by magic but by the transforming activities of living into fluency in the "new world" gifted to the believer by God's gracious inclusion of him or her into the faith community. In short, God's grace is the light that brings dawn upon "another quality of consciousness." Holmer continues:

> Faith of the Abrahamic sort is a new move for the consciousness itself. It asks that a subject project himself, make sense of his

life, ... to establish a kind of criterion, to make a certainty, by a community with God himself.[75]

Holmer is not disregarding creedal subscription. However, the kind of truth-as-objectivity found in allegiance to creedal statements is stillborn unless accompanied by what Kierkegaard called truth-as-subjectivity (not merely "Jesus is Lord" but "Jesus is *my* Lord"). In another important passage Holmer writes that faith

is not a matter of having a doctrine about the sentences of religion and ethics as much as it is a matter of disposing oneself properly, being the proper "I" or subject; hence it becomes a matter of deploying correctly the concepts involved. This correlation calls for a re-ordering of one's dispositions regarding the sentences, the "how" again, and not a new set of sentences or a meta-explanation or translation of those teachings.[76]

Holmer is emphasizing that truth-as-subjectivity necessarily involves meta-projection of oneself into the world of Scripture.

In addition to reading oneself into the Scriptural text, projecting oneself back into the New Testament world as it were, grammatical fluency in the living faith also involves projecting the New Testament world into the present. Think again of the typical rendering of 2 Cor. 5:17, "If anyone is in Christ, that one is a new creature." What does this newness entail? New standing, for one is forgiven. Is that all? Also a new inheritance, eternal life. New certainty. New dispositions. New desires. New family. New language. And so on! It doesn't take much thought to realize that there cannot be a new me unless everything around me is shot through with new meaning and new significance. In short: it is a whole new world (*kainē ktisis*).

Holmer details the dual projection—me into Scripture, and Scripture into the present—in terms of three sorts of "means." Before we can enumerate these, we must be careful to catch what Holmer is envisioning. Admittedly, to call them "means" is a little misleading. For Holmer "means" do not stand to "ends" as "cause" stands to "effect" (what philosophers call "external, or causal, relation"). Rather, means stands to ends as *constitutive* of the ends; or again, means and ends are *internally* related. Projection is not the how-to that achieves something else. Rather, the projecting is itself the point and end point. How does this work?

We think, speak, act, desire (etc.) *from* rather than *to* a form of life. And while much of our form of life is shared, to say that humans share the aspect of subjectivity is something that is also unique to each person. Said differently, our shared form of life includes the first-person singular (even though my first-person singular is obviously different from yours). "My thinking and talking is, for me as for you (in the first person) the very means of achieving and establishing, projecting and describing those facets of life."[77] In other words, the end goal is attained progressively as the skills that constitute the end goal are learned in the struggle to project myself into the text and project the text into the present. No one can do this for me. *I* must do it for me. Yet I cannot do it in isolation. *I* must do it, but I can only do it with others on the same journey.[78]

Holmer is not easily understood. I think he means something like the following: If the world is constituted by language, as Wittgenstein maintains, then the "means" to a new world, a new life, is a new language. The new language cannot be delivered to me like a UPS parcel. Nor can it be learned by reading translations. A new language means acquiring and developing new set of skills. One needs to learn how to "go on" (i.e., how to project in new contexts).[79] This does not come easily. It comes by doing. In Wittgenstein's words, "We are engaged in a *struggle* with language" and likewise, "if you want to stay within the religious sphere, you must *struggle*."[80] There is no time in this life when the struggle is over. Just as the means to the end of "being a friend" is "being a friend," so too the struggle toward fluency is simultaneously the means *and* the end, namely fluency in the new language.

What then are these end-constituting means? Holmer enumerates three sorts of means, each of which are constitutive of the end of meta-projection: (a) literary, (b) nonliterary, and

(c) relational. Perhaps it is clearer to refer to them as lessons to be learned in the school of projection.

a. Literary Means

Christianity is at once "surprisingly plain and infinitely supple."[81] As a result of this suppleness, theology involves interpretation that is highly nuanced. By "nuance" Holmer doesn't mean "hair-splitting"—though of course theology doesn't disregard fine-grained logical distinctions. But meta-projection does not end with logical consistency.

> I say again that theology has to be projected. The literary means have always been metaphors, parables, stories, informal conversation, everyday speech, allegories, and a rich use of vivifying materials. This is not to argue for chalk talks, buzz sessions, or tea groups; but one of the reasons these, too, arise is that theology is never perfectly done in syllogisms, arguments and processes of verified reporting.[82]

The "vivifying" materials are the parts of narrative that logic-choppers are quick to lop off as too fuzzy or imprecise to be considered. But to become fluent in the thought forms of the New Testament requires deep immersion into the fuzzy stuff: into the parables, stories, metaphors, and figures. Therein is skill deeply formed.

When Mozart died, his *Requiem* was played at his own funeral Mass. Unfortunately, the work was not finished at the time of his death, and it fell to his "grad students" to complete the work. The year I wrote this essay, the choirs of the Dayton Philharmonic Orchestra performed two versions of the *Requiem*: the commonly heard ending, composed in 1792 by Mozart's star pupil, Franz Xaver Süssmayr; and a twenty-first-century completion by a consortium of six American composers that goes by the name "Sleeping Giant." It is a live question whose projection is "better." Projection requires creative imagination by composers aiming to complete the *Requiem*. Phrase-by-phrase same-saying will not do the trick. Nor can poetic liberties by would-be completers be taken "too far" or no one will recognize it as a completion of *Mozart's* work. The central aim is what might be termed "satisfactory fit." A successful projection must achieve dynamic or functional similarity, which is to say that the new score must perform work analogous to the original, but in the twenty-first-century rather than eighteenth-century Austria.[83] So too for theology. Theological projection that "fits" must perform a similar function as the original—namely immerse one into a living language and cultural fluency.[84]

b. Nonliterary Means

The second lesson to be learned at the school of projection involves *non*-literary means. One doesn't master a language by memorizing flash cards. Rather, the new language must permeate the whole of active living. In the context of discussing Kierkegaard's *Fear and Trembling*, Holmer wrote

> of a deep kind of understanding that is projected for us by the same book [Kierkegaard's *Fear and Trembling*]. But it is projected and cannot be delivered to us. For it requires a *deep kind of activity*. If one becomes faithful, then one's consciousness of oneself is moved by the wanting, wishing, and caring that made Abraham faithful and the father of faith. By so doing, one surely would also know God. Within that decisiveness, a new rule, a new life, a new understanding would ensue.[85]

"Deep kind of activity" is not activity on one occasion only. There can be no gaining of fluency without *ongoing* activity. "Though we can learn about God from the bible, we are also expected to become learners, to learn as we go, from living in accord with Jesus, and with Apostolic faithfulness in mind. Our walking by faith is also an ongoing learning about God."[86] For example, the grammar of "forgive" includes ongoing "deep activities" such as surrendering grudges, absorbing unjust costs, and smiling away insults.

c. Relational Means

Third, projection necessarily involves learning lessons comprised of a relational component.

> The [projective] imagination I refer to is .... the outworking of the language *about* faith when it becomes the language *of* faith. It moves from being like a grammar to being solicitous, personal, and persuasive. One cannot be solicitous without being imaginative, for solicitude demands that we have sympathy—pathos *with and for others*. We cannot do that unless we project others unto ourselves as God's children, a real and as worthy as we are and maybe more .... Those parables and metaphors [esp. Mt 25] are not decoration and little literary graces added to the hard facts. Rather, those strange little imaginative projections are the very means by which love will well up in us and the grace of God grip us with heartiness.[87]

Once again, the passional changes that a person undergoes in becoming a person of faith involve a shift of emphasis away from "truth-as-objectivity" to "truth-as-subjectivity." Truth-as-objectivity may actually stymie the faith of the philosophical skeptic seeking ever more evidence, because "objective" evidence pales into insignificance next to the invitation to join up with others on the Way.

> Furthermore, once the talk of using them [i.e., Christian concepts, sentences, stories, and teachings] as projective possibilities and possible ways of living life begins, the entire

issue respecting their objective truth or falsity begins to change too. The logic remains the same; i.e., relative to the canons of history, metaphysics and other kinds of descriptive language they remain objectively uncertain. But a thinker no longer lets the objective uncertainty keep him from believing. A man begins to want to believe them, and his certitude about them grows up with the passage of time and the strenuousness of his ethico-religious striving .... It is clear now that the stress upon the necessity of the "how" is, of course, a measure of the concern with reality and also with the truth as subjectivity.[88]

The kind of "certainty" of which Holmer speaks here is grammatical (i.e., criterial). It is the kind of certainty one experiences when instinctively employing the just-right word for the occasion (e.g., "wet" while standing in the rain). And attaining grammatical certainty necessarily involves behind-the-scenes community.

When St. Paul instructs the church at Philippi to behave as befits the Gospel, each of the pronouns is in the second-person plural. Paul addresses them as if they were one corporate person:

Only let your [pl.] *conversation* [Gk. *politeuomai*] be as it becometh the gospel of Christ: that whether I come and see you [pl.], or else be absent, I may hear of your [pl.] affairs, that ye [pl.] stand fast in one spirit, with one mind striving together for the faith of the gospel.[89]

I cite the King James Version because of its striking choice of words. Surprising to me in this instance, KJV is closer to the Greek than modern translations. In 1611, the English word "conversation" denoted "the action of consorting or having dealings with others; living together; commerce, intercourse, society, intimacy," in short "having one's being in a place or among persons." So says the *Oxford English Dictionary*. On the other hand, the Greek term it translates is *politeuomai*, a cognate of the term for community, *polis*, from which we get the familiar Minnea*polis* and *politics*. As a verb, *politeuomai* means to conduct ourselves—together in the plural—as a healthy community. (And here we do well to remember that "community" derives directly from the Latin *co* + *munus*, literally a "shared world.") While individual free agency is involved, the idea of the verb is that of a complex weaving of individuals into a communal whole, into a shared world. The shape of the intra-communal "conversation"—both dealings and dialogue—is one of the ways Wittgenstein used the phrase "form of life," the complicated interweaving of all the grammars—of "chair" and "to feed."[90] Deepening one's fluency in this form of life is the road we travel to become friends of each other and of God.

For Holmer, theology done well contributes to a believer's fluency.

> The knowledge of God does not get moved from one mind to another in a direct and immediate way .... By themselves [theological writings] are not the matters called "knowing God"; but they are like a grammar and like a means with which you, the reader, come to know God. "Knowing God" is not done on paper. One must think about this by way of getting to know a person.[91]

Here we see how Holmer's concept of *meta-projection* differs even from the geometer's search for the inscribed heptadecagon. What distinguishes mathematics is that one can take the problem and solve it at a distance.[92] But not so with theological projection. Theological projection involves a person in a King James "conversation" which is to say, dealings and dialogues with compatriots in a particular time and place. And one of those compatriots is God Himself.

> [A]ppreciation and approval of the news are not the sufficient response, any more than hearty endorsement of grammatical rules or swearing allegiance to logical requisites are enough. No, we must become grammatical in speaking about everything else, not the grammar, before those rules have been really understood. So too, it is of little use to be logical

about logic when the point is that we are supposed to have learned to become logical about whatever we think. This is how it is, then, with theology—namely, that we are to become Godly in all things, referring everything, our woes and weal, fears and joys, past and future, completely to God's love and care.[93]

Theological projection is personal, invasive even, because you and I cannot become whole persons until every nook and cranny of our "conversation" is permeated by the world-constituting-language of God.

Conclusion

I began this essay claiming that Holmer's theology is deeply indebted to Wittgenstein. I defended this claim by showing the presence of a single technical term that Holmer imports from Wittgenstein: "Theology must be *projected*." We know that a baseball can be projected out of the park. And moving pictures can be projected onto the silver screen. There is no mystery with these examples. But how is theology to be projected? Let me recap with some practical lessons.

I have argued that for Holmer, as for Wittgenstein, projection is a function of lived skills. Of course, Giancarlo Stanton was skilled when he hit the ball out of Dodger stadium. And Thomas Edison was skilled when he invented the Kinetograph. But in both these cases, fans who were unskilled would have been able to envision both projections—the huge homerun and the moving picture—before they witnessed the events.

But some projections are more elusive by nature such that only the highly trained can recognize a projection when they see one. Only the highly skilled can spot an endgame in chess as *elegant* in advance of the checkmate, an unorthodox procedure as an *advance* in medicine, or a variation of a musical score as *fitting*.

What hinders theological projection, then, is anything that discounts or dismisses the need for hard-won growth in skill, aka godliness.[94] When Holmer set out to assess contemporary attempts at theological projection, he discovered four things that have clogged up the works. The first involves our tendency to fixate on words rather than on message:

> [T]he words of the bible are like words anywhere: they are only meaningful and say something when they are conceived to belong to speakers, to situations, to occasions. Words do not mean; they do not say; people mean and something or other with them.[95]

But many well-meaning Christians are prone to see the Bible as a magical artifact.

> Instead of exploring that book in the interest of the blinding light that God will bring, it is as if the whole

book must be praised, massaged by some phrases, and its message summarized and encapsulated for a more ready consumption.[96]

As a result, theological projection is thwarted.

The second obstacle to projection is the human penchant for thinking in terms of facts instead of grammar. We cannot expect to "google" the answer to "What does faithfulness to the Gospel entail today?" The *form* the answer to *this* question inevitably takes is not that of (biblical) factoids but rather a set of tips, reminders, and hints regarding how to go on from where we are. It is the sort of thing that might be offered by a spiritual coach, sage, or prophet. Wittgenstein saw his primary role as one of "assembling reminders for a particular purpose" rather than "advancing theses."[97] So too Holmer sees St. Paul in writing to Christians in Corinth says "something that is true and that is startling: however, it is more like a reflective comment, a reminder made about the very morphology and logic of the gospel itself."[98] Like a coach, there is no advice in general for theologians to offer, but only the sort of flesh and blood coaching that begins precisely where a given athlete is. In this way, Holmer understands the task of the theological projector much like that of the language coach.

Holmer notes a third obstacle to theological projection in our craving for overly tidy simplifications. When painting the morning mist on a lake, the artist does not imitate a child's coloring book and outline the "edges" of the fog in black! The boundaries of mist are fuzzy, not clearly defined. So too theology: the logic (i.e., grammar) of Christian believing is not something that can be spelled out simply or clearly enough so as to be mass-produced for general consumption. Or to recall the former illustration, faithful representation is not akin to a film shown to a new audience night after night (aka *Vorstellung*). Rather, it is like a *re*-presentation (aka *Darstellung*) of, say, Shakespeare's Julius Caesar in San Quentin Prison.[99] In the first case, a high school dropout can turn on the film projector while everyone sits back and consumes popcorn. But changes of venue in the second case make enormous demands on the actors who are themselves *living* projectors. So too for Christian believing; the demands upon the would-be projectors are very high and very personal.

> If one asked, "When does one believe?" the answers are terrifyingly multiplex but also tellingly simple. It seems that one cannot be believing if one does not love; and believing in God is not evinced if one has not done his commandments. On the contrary, believing in a treacherous and superficial way is castigated by the thought that the evil one can also believe—but without any of the above noted features.[100]

The fourth obstacle Holmer perceives to projecting theology arises when sincere Christians are bewitched by "philosophical theism." Holmer's allusion is to Pascal's *Le Mémorial* (sewn into the lining of his coat and discovered after he died) in which he confesses a burning personal faith in the God of Abraham, Isaac, and Jacob but decidedly *not* in the god of the philosophers and scholars.[101] Space prohibits me from detailing the complex history of this bewitchment.[102] But the basic issue for Holmer is whether we get to know God by an exercise of metaphysical analysis of the content of the Bible or more simply by learning how to talk *of* God, and *with* God, well and with confidence.[103]

> It seems to me obvious enough that there is something very wrong, if not truly nonsensical, in thinking that the religion of the New Testament could have a foundation at all in anything like a philosophical scheme or metaphysical reality.
>
> . . .
>
> The Bible asks for something so different. It demands a kind of trust in God and a kind of fear of him. Arguments do not do that.[104]

Although Holmer spells out four obstacles to performing the maxim "Theology must be projected," Holmer never does describe in positive steps or recipe for *how* to project theology in contemporary culture. This may be disappointing, for we all hanker after sure-fire techniques. Yet Holmer insists:

To believe in God does not mean holding views about him nor is it a matter of getting to know him the way one gets to know physics or archaeology. God is not knowable or believable like that. If I believe in God, then I say: "Thou art the Lord," I give up a lot of fretting and vain trying, and rejoice in him.[105]

To believe in God is decidedly *not* an epistemic exercise

Holmer's ideas about theological projection may be somewhat more plausible if we call to mind how wonderful and surprising it is when children learn to speak. We *live* with children, we *speak* to each other within earshot of the child, we *play* with children, we *care* for children. And all of a sudden, they are talking! Theological projection is just that: the ordinary but highly ramified and lifelong matter of faithfully speaking, living and loving in the presence of the next generation.

Notes

1 Paul Holmer, *The Grammar of Faith* (San Francisco, CA: Harper and Row Publishers, 1978), 26. Below I will argue that, properly understood, theological projection is really a case of *meta*-projection. Not that this pretentious label makes anything clearer. But for Holmer, theological projection is not simply a first-order enterprise, but a second-order one.

2 Paul L. Holmer, "Truth Is Subjectivity: Some Logical Considerations," in *On Kierkegaard and the Truth*, ed. David J. Gouwers and Lee C. Barrett III (Cambridge, UK: James Clark & Co., 2012), 144. Emphasis added.

3 Wittgenstein visited Malcolm in Ithaca in 1949. Cornell University houses one of two facsimile copies of Wittgenstein's *Nachlaß*. Until recent electronic distribution, the only other copy in the United States was on the West coast, housed in the graduate library of UCLA.

4 Norman Malcolm, *Ludwig Wittgenstein: A Memoir with a Biographical Sketch by G. H. Von Wright; Second Edition with Wittgenstein's Letters to Malcolm* (Oxford: Clarendon, 1958, 2001), 106–7.

5 It should be noted that *Concluding Unscientific Postscript* was Kierkegaard's last pseudonymous work. After 1843, Kierkegaard no longer wrote "indirect discourse," but in "direct discourse," writing about Christian believing no longer as an outsider but as an explicitly religious author. Such "direct discourse" works include *Training for Christianity*, *Edifying Discourses*, and *Works of Love*. For an account of Kierkegaard's "metamorphosis" after 1847 see Walter Lowrie, *A Short Life of Kierkegaard* (Princeton, NJ: Princeton University Press, 1942).

6 As told by David Cain in "Afterword," Paul L. Holmer, *On Kierkegaard and the Truth*, ed. David J. Gouwens and Lee C. Barrett III, The Paul L. Holmer Papers (Cambridge & Eugene, OR: James Clarke & Cascade Books, 2012), 165.

7 Ludwig Wittgenstein, *Culture and Value: A Selection from the Posthumous Remains*, ed. G. H. von Wright and Heikki Nyman, trans. Peter Winch; second edition revised by Alois Pichler (Oxford, UK: Basil Blackwell, 1998), 24. See my "Wittgenstein: I can't believe ... yet." [Forthcoming].

8 Ray Monk, *Ludwig Wittgenstein: The Duty of Genius* (New York: Viking Penguin, 1990), 527.

9 MS 183, the so-called Koder diaries, have been translated, Ludwig Wittgenstein, *Ludwig Wittgenstein: Public and Private Occasions*

(Lanham, MD: Rowman & Littlefield, 2003). On the public confessions see Monk, *Ludwig Wittgenstein: The Duty of Genius*, 361–84.

10 By "constitutes" I do not mean materially constitutive, as a leaf pile is nothing but a collection of individual leaves. I mean rather that the two are internally related. Wittgenstein once said "The limit of language is shown by its being impossible to describe the fact which corresponds to (is the translation of) a sentence, without simply repeating the sentence." Wittgenstein, *Culture and Value*, 13e. In other words, we have no nonlinguistic criteria to affirm or deny the correspondence of a sentence and a state of affairs. There is no nonlinguistic standpoint from which we can make such an assessment.

11 Luther *Bibel*, Jn 1:1.

12 Martin Buber, *Ich Und Du* (Leipzig: Reclam Philipp Jun, 1995 [1933]), 24.

13 *Faust, Part I*, cited in Wittgenstein, *Culture and Value*, 36.

14 "In a conversation: One person throws a ball; the other does not know: is he to throw it back, throw it to a third person, or leave it lying, or pick it up & put it in his pocket, etc." Ibid., 84.

15 See the motley list given in Ludwig Wittgenstein, *Philosophical Investigations*, ed. G. E. M. Anscombe and Rush Rhees, trans. G. E. M. Anscombe (New York: Macmillan, 1953), §23.

16 Ibid., §§11–12, etc.

17 "For a large class of cases—though not for all—in which we employ the word 'meaning' it can be defined thus: the meaning of a word is its use in the language." Ibid., §43.

18 Bertrand Russell, "Appearance and Reality," in *The Problems of Philosophy* (London: Oxford University Press, 1959), 11. Emphasis added.

19 Wittgenstein once wrote, "One man is a convinced realist, another is a convinced idealist and teaches his children accordingly. In such an important matter as the existence or non-existence of the external world they don't want to teach their children anything wrong." Ludwig

Wittgenstein, *Zettel*, ed. G. E. M. Anscombe and G. H. von Wright, trans. G. E. M. Anscombe (Berkeley and Los Angeles: University of California Press, 1970), §413. Clearly Wittgenstein was not interested in arguing out whether realism or nonrealism was more rational than the other. His concern lay with the way our language use *shows* the sort of "realism" that is worth troubling about.

20 *Remarks on the Foundations of Mathematics*, ed. G. H. von Wright, Rush Rhees, and G. E. M. Anscombe, trans. G. E. M. Anscombe (Cambridge, MA and London, UK: MIT Press, 1978), VI.23

21 *Philosophical Investigations*, §381.

22 In an early entry, Wittgenstein wrote, that "the limits of *the* language (the language which I understand) mean the limits of *my* world." *Tractatus* 5.62. And while it is true that one's "world" grows as one's language expands, but Wittgenstein later rejected the image because (1) the boundaries or limits [*Grenzen*] of the "world" are unspecifiable and (2) because the use of the image tempts us to think that one might imagine it is possible to think the other side of the "limit." But "beyond" in this context is pure gibberish. James Conant and Cora Diamond, "On Reading the Tractatus Resolutely," in *Wittgenstein's Lasting Significance*, ed. Max Kölbel and Bernhard Weiss (London: Routledge, 2004), 46–99.

23 Norman Malcolm, *Ludwig Wittgenstein: A Memoir* (London: Oxford University Press, 1958), 69.

24 Wittgenstein, *Zettel*, §227.

25 *Remarks on the Foundations of Mathematics*, VI §48, p. 352. Emphasis added.

26 Ludwig Wittgenstein, *The Blue and Brown Books* (New York: Harper and Brothers, 1958), 24.

27 See *Philosophical Investigations*, §116. "When philosophers use a word ... and try to grasp the essence of the thing, one must always ask oneself: is the word ever actually used in this way in the language-game which is its original home?—What *we* do is to bring words back from their metaphysical to their everyday use."

28 William Kingdon Clifford, "The Ethics of Belief," in *The Ethics of Belief and Other Essays* (Amherst, NY: Prometheus, 2009 [1877]), 94.

29 Sean Illing, "9 Questions for Neil Degrasse Tyson; the Astrophysicist on Curiosity, Bad Intellectual Habits, and Reading National Review.," *Vox* (March 25, 2017), http://www.vox.com/convers ations/2017/3/25/14986946/9-questions-neil-degrasse-tyson-science-national-review. http://www.vox.com/conversatio ns/2017/3/25/14986946/9-questions-neil-degrasse-tyson-science-national-review

30 As I understand the discussion throughout the *Investigations*, criteria are internally related to what Wittgenstein calls "grammar," a seminal notion that first shows up in 1931. For discussion see Cora Diamond, "Does Bismark Have a Beetle in His Box?," in *The New Wittgenstein*, ed. Alice Crary and Rupert Read (New York: Routledge, 2000), 262–92.

31 Wittgenstein, *Philosophical Investigations*, §§354, 55.

32 E.g., "In order for hope to be projected, language must already be in place." Paul L. Holmer, "Wittgenstein and Kierkegaard: The Subjective Thinker," in *Thinking the Faith with Passion: Selected Essays*, ed. David J. Gouwers and Lee C. Barrett III (Cambridge, UK: James Clark & Co., 2012), 82.

33 Wittgenstein, *Philosophical Investigations*, §373.

34 In the first half of the twentieth century, verification by the five senses was the preferred method for establishing the truth or falsity of claims, aka logical positivism.

35 Wittgenstein, *Philosophical Investigations*, §33.

36 Ibid., §142.

37 Holmer, *The Grammar of Faith*, 19.

38 Ibid., 22.

39 Holmer, "About Being a Person: Kierkegaard's *Fear and Trembling*," 71–2.

40 Wittgenstein, *Philosophical Investigations*, §§241, 42.

41 *Remarks on the Foundations of Mathematics*, I §116. Emphasis added.

42 The word "converted" is Holmer's own. "Nothing whatsoever is wrong with that old knowledge of God. We do not have to make it new. It is the recipient who has to be revivified and converted." Holmer, *The Grammar of Faith*, 36. Holmer's point in using the term "converted" is not to take a side on the issue of whether a child can or cannot be slowly educated into the faith or whether "conversion" must be dramatic, as was the case of St. Paul. Rather, it is the totality of the life change that is in view. For both the child and St. Paul, conversion names the fact that change comes from the outside the person—by means of a gift, or grace—and fluently inhabiting the "new world" is not simply a matter of vocabulary acquisition but of *lived* fluency. In "Learning to Theologise," Holmer wrote, "Christians are convinced that we all need to be re-born, that we need to be radically re-oriented to everyday life and the flow of our experience" (195). This can happen in several ways. But the hoped for end, and that which is the focus of this present essay, happens when "we can re-duplicate the lives of Christians, adopt the Christian form of life, and then, language of faith becomes our language. When one becomes at home in it, it begins to mean something, for it is tied up with so much else in one's life" (200). See Paul L. Holmer, "Learning to Theologise," in *Wittgenstein: Attention to Particulars: Essays in Honour of Rush* Rhees *(1905–89)*, ed. D.Z. Phillips (New York and Frankfurt am Main: St. Martin's Press and Suhrkamp, 1989), 194–200.

43 *Ei tis en Christō, kainē ktisis.* 2 Cor. 5:17.

44 Acts 9:1-19.

45 2 Cor. 5:16, "Therefore from now on we recognize no one according to the flesh."

46 1 Cor. 3:1-2. (St. Peter repeats the image of "baby," 1 Pe. 2:2.) Another important Pauline image is that of rescue from the kingdom of darkness and transfer of citizenship into the kingdom of God's Son. Col. 1:12-13.

47 Holmer, *The Grammar of Faith*, 18–19. Emphasis added.

48 Ibid., 19.

49 Ibid., 20.

50 Ibid., 24. Emphasis added.

51 Ibid., 23. Emphasis added.

52 Ibid., 26. Emphasis added.

53 Ibid., 26–7.

54 Søren Kierkegaard, *Purity of Heart Is to Will One Thing; Spiritual Preparation for the Office of Confession* (San Francisco: HarperCollins, 1948 [1847]).

55 Ludwig Wittgenstein, *Wittgenstein's Lectures on the Foundations of Mathematics. Cambridge, 1939: From the Notes of R. G. Bosanquet, Norman Malcolm, Rush Rhees, and Yorick Smythies*, ed. Cora Diamond, (Chicago: University of Chicago Press, 1975), 240.

56 Brad J. Kallenberg, "Rethinking Fideism through the Lens of Wittgenstein's Engineering Outlook," *International Journal for the Philosophy of Religion* 71, no. 1 (2012): 55–73.

57 Wittgenstein, *Wittgenstein's Lectures on the Foundations of Mathematics*, 69. Emphasis added.

58 For further discussion by Wittgenstein, see *Philosophical Grammar*, ed. Rush Rhees, trans. Anthony Kenny (Berkeley and Los Angeles: University of California Press, 1974), 204–5.

59 *Philosophical Investigations*, Pt. 2 p. 291.

60 29 March, 1976 cover of *The New Yorker*. http://juliasantengallery.com/wp-content/uploads/2012/12/New-Yorker-2306.jpg

61 Initial subway maps were correlated with the above-ground streets, but no one could use the maps! Jonathan Z. Smith, *Relating Religion* (Chicago and London: The University of Chicago Press, 2004), 59–60.

62 Daniel E. Hall, "The Guild of Surgeons as a Tradition of Moral Enquiry," *Journal of Medicine and Philosophy* 34 (2011): 114–32.

63 Wittgenstein, *Wittgenstein's Lectures on the Foundations of Mathematics*, 19.

64 For discussion see ibid., 63–86.

65 For help envisioning a heptadecagon, see https://en.wikipedia.org/wiki/File:Regular_polygon_17_annotated.svg.

66 For example, see http://mathpages.com/home/kmath487.htm.

67 Holmer, *The Grammar of Faith*, 31. And Holmer, "Truth Is Subjectivity," 144.

68 Stanley Cavell, *The Claim of Reason: Wittgenstein, Skepticism, Morality, and Tragedy* (New York: Oxford University Press, 1999 [1979]), 181.

69 Ibid. Emphasis added.

70 Ibid.

71 Ibid., 122.

72 Projecting oneself back into the Scriptural world has been described by Holmer's colleague at Yale, Hans Frei. See Hans Frei, *The Eclipse of Biblical Narrative: A Study in Eighteenth- and Nineteenth-Century Hermeneutics* (New Haven, CT: Yale University Press, 1974).

73 Holmer, *The Grammar of Faith*, 29–30.

74 Ibid., 27.

75 Holmer, "About Being a Person: Kierkegaard's *Fear and Trembling*," 71.

76 Holmer, "Truth Is Subjectivity," 144.

77 Holmer, "Wittgenstein and Kierkegaard," 83.

78 "Shun youthful passions and pursue righteousness, faith, love, and peace, along *with* those who call on the Lord from a pure heart." 2 Tim. 2:22.

79 For Wittgenstein's discussion of understanding as knowing how to "go on," see Wittgenstein, *Philosophical Investigations*, §§151–5. Emphasis added.

80 Wittgenstein, *Culture and Value*, 98. Emphasis added.

81 Holmer, *The Grammar of Faith*, 22.

82 Ibid., 26–7.

83 For Wittgenstein on dynamic similarity see Brad J. Kallenberg, "Dynamical Similarity and the Problem of Evil," in *God, Grace and Creation: The Annual Publication of the College Theology Society 2009, Vol. 55*, ed. Philip J. Rossi (Maryknoll, NY: Orbis Press, 2010), 163–83.

84 Consider the Clarence Jordan's "Cotton Patch Gospel" that resets the story of the Good Samaritan in the deep South, a compassionate black man taking the place of the kind-hearted Samaritan. Clarence Jordan, *Cotton Patch Version of Luke and Acts* (Clinton: New Win Publishing, 1969), 46–7.

85 Holmer, "About Being a Person: Kierkegaard's *Fear and Trembling*," 76. Emphasis added.

86 Holmer, *The Grammar of Faith*, 24.

87 Ibid., 27. Emphasis added.

88 Holmer, "Truth Is Subjectivity," 144–5.

89 Phil 1:27, KJV.

90 Wittgenstein, *Philosophical Investigations*, §241.

91 Holmer, *The Grammar of Faith*, 31–2.

92 "Suppose I say ….'Project the circle in a certain way' … If it is a mathematical task, you can go away and do it elsewhere; you can do this [projection] anywhere." Wittgenstein, *Wittgenstein's Lectures on the Foundations of Mathematics*, 84.

93 Holmer, *The Grammar of Faith*, 19.

94 "Theology … must be absorbed, and when it is, the hearer is supposed to become Godly." Ibid., 18–19.

95 Paul Holmer, "Contemporary Evangelical Faith: An Assessment and Critique," in *The Evangelicals: What They Believe, Who They Are, Where They Are Changing*, ed. David F. Wells and John D. Woodbridge (Grand Rapids, MI: Baker, 1977), 72. The label in the title of this essay, "evangelical," in 1977 did not mean what it means now some forty years later. In Germany, "evangelical" simply meant "Protestant" or more specifically, "Lutheran." Granted, Holmer is Lutheran, but he is American rather than German, so by the term Holmer means something other than merely "Lutheran." For our purposes, "evangelical" means those sorts of Christians who take the Bible very seriously. Their seriousness culminated in a declaration of biblical inerrancy. The International Council on Biblical Inerrancy (ICBI) was held in Chicago in October 1978, on which occasion approximately 200 self-designated evangelical leaders formulated the "Chicago Statement on Biblical Inerrancy." As to the identity of American "evangelicals" *c.* 1977, see Donald W. Dayton, "*Discovering an Evangelical Heritage*," (San Francisco, CA: Harper & Row, 1976).

96 Holmer, "Contemporary Evangelical Faith," 74.

97 Wittgenstein, *Philosophical Investigations*, §§127–8.

98 Holmer, "Contemporary Evangelical Faith," 74–5.

99 Cp. Sean Elder, "Why They're Doing Shakespeare in Prison," *Newsweek* (December 11, 2016).

100 Holmer, "Contemporary Evangelical Faith," 81. Internal biblical allusions are to 1 John 2:3-11 (etc.) and Jas. 2:19.

101 There are many online images of this document in French and Latin with English translations.

102 Compare the skepticism of Kenny with the optimism of Plantinga. Anthony Kenny, *The God of the Philosophers* (Oxford, UK: Clarendon, 1987). James F. Sennett, ed. *The Analytic Theist: An Alvin Plantinga Reader* (Grand Rapids, MI: Eerdmans, 1998).

103 Holmer, "Contemporary Evangelical Faith," 91–2.

104 Ibid., 92.

105 Ibid., 94.

3

Paul Holmer and the Religious Interpretation of Kierkegaard

Anders Kraal

Paul Holmer is one of the foremost twentieth-century North American representatives of what could be called the Religious Interpretation of Kierkegaard. According to this interpretation, Kierkegaard was not primarily a proto-existentialist, a theorist of radical choice, or a talented literary craftsman with philosophical interests, but a religious, or more specifically a Christian, thinker, whose philosophical project, interests, and aims were decisively shaped by his commitments to the Christian religion as he understood it. In what follows I offer an intellectual genealogy of Holmer's reading of Kierkegaard, and in so doing I also offer part of the intellectual genealogy of the Religious Interpretation of Kierkegaard more generally. I outline some core features of this interpretation, and then trace these features back to David F. Swenson of the University of Minnesota, and from Swenson to Waldemar Rudin and Torsten Bohlin of Uppsala University in Sweden.

I. Holmer's Kierkegaard Interpretation

Central to Holmer's Kierkegaard interpretation, then, is the insistence that Kierkegaard was fundamentally a Christian thinker. This comes out already in his early piece "Kierkegaard and Theology" (1957), in which he takes Kierkegaard's main philosophical task to have been that of "reintroducing Christianity into Christendom."[1] The theme persisted throughout Holmer's literary career. In his posthumous *On Kierkegaard and the Truth* (2012), he says of Kierkegaard that "[t]he evangelical hope of bringing the reader face to face with the God of Jesus Christ never forsakes him for a moment," that "the purpose governing his literature is finally to provide the reader the opportunity of seeing what Christianity is," and that Kierkegaard should be understood as "a Christian philosopher" who "believes the Scriptural account and ... does not believe the grand systematic philosophical accounts."[2]

Holmer sought to flesh out the nature of Kierkegaard's Christian philosophizing primarily via reference to Kierkegaard's central idea that *truth is subjectivity*. Kierkegaard had introduced this idea at the end of *Either/Or*, where he ascribes it to a minister whose sermon "The Upbuilding That Lies in the Thought That in Relation to God We are Always in the Wrong" was found by Victor Eremita in the papers of Author B.[3] The minister asks his listeners (or readers) whether the evil they suffer unjustly makes them want to think that they have been wronged by God, or instead that they are in the wrong against God in feeling this way. The minister then goes on to urge to not stop short of an answer to this question, an answer that is both deep and true for them, for "only the truth which edifies is *true for you*" (my emphasis).[4] The idea of something being "true for you," or subjectively true, was later taken up for elaborate discussion in the *Concluding Unscientific Postscript* (1846), where it is formulated as the thesis that "truth is subjectivity."[5]

Holmer offers an exposition and discussion of the claim that "truth is subjectivity" in his *Kierkegaard and the Truth*, where it is argued:

> Kierkegaard considered his definition [of truth as subjectivity] commensurable both with the nature of logic and with the claim that Jesus Christ is the truth … *and is his attempt to*

> *state the character of Christianity in philosophical terms which do not essentially modify it.*[6]

Holmer elaborates:

> [Kierkegaard] sought clarity ... on what was to him the highest and most important knowledge, Christianity ... The claim that Christ is the truth, mark the words, not speaks the truth but is the truth, sets the problem for Kierkegaard. His many volumes are written with this as the guiding star ... his philosophy of religion argues really from the existence of Jesus Christ, or rather, it presupposes His existence and seeks to explicate the meaning of His existence.[7]

So, Holmer takes Kierkegaard to be a religious thinker whose core ideas should be understood within a decisively Christian framework. In what follows I argue that this approach should be understood as an application of a basic claim of Holmer's teacher Swenson's Kierkegaard interpretation.

II. The Swensonian Background

Holmer claims in *On Kierkegaard and the Truth* that he would be "neither surprised nor disappointed" if his book was considered "Swensonian."[8] In his early Yale dissertation, *Kierkegaard and the truth* (1946), he had gone even further, characterizing his Kierkegaard interpretation as "unashamedly Swensonian."[9]

David Swenson, a first-generation Swedish immigrant, spent his entire academic career at the University of Minnesota, advancing from Instructor (1901–6) to Assistant Professor (1906–13) to Associate Professor (1913–17) to full Professor (1917–40). He had discovered Kierkegaard by stumbling upon *Concluding Unscientific Postscript* while browsing in a Scandinavian immigrant library in Minneapolis in 1900,[10] and had subsequently made it his chief academic mission to introduce Kierkegaard to North American academia. He was fairly successful in this: his lectures on Kierkegaard at the University of Minnesota in the 1910s were the first Kierkegaard lectures ever delivered at a North American university; his paper "The Anti-Intellectualism of Kierkegaard," published in *The Philosophical Review* in 1917, was the first Kierkegaard article to appear in a North American philosophy journal; his translations of Kierkegaard's *Philosophical Fragments* and *Concluding Unscientific Postscript*, published by Princeton University Press in 1936 and 1941, respectively, were the first English translations of these texts to be published by a North American university press. Moreover, Swenson's *Something about Kierkegaard* (1941) has acquired the status of a classic in North American Kierkegaard Studies.[11]

Swenson came from a religious family, and remained religious throughout his life.[12] According to Swenson's former students and colleagues at the University of Minnesota, it was the specifically Christian character of Kierkegaard's thought that attracted Swenson to Kierkegaard. Mary Carmen Rose, a former student, recalls that "Swenson never lost sight ... of Kierkegaard's avowal that he wrote out of the depth of his own ever developing and deepening Christian commitment."[13] George P. Conger, a former colleague, recalls that Swenson regarded Kierkegaard as "my philosopher" and derived from him "major reinforcement of his religious faith."[14] More recently, David Gouwens and Lee C. Barrett III claim that "Swenson's Kierkegaard was no extreme anti-rationalist but rather a Christian philosopher whose work implicitly suggested that belief in a transcendent source of meaning is a legitimate response to the ambiguity and anguish of human life."[15]

I believe Gouwens and Barrett III are by and large correct in characterizing Swenson's understanding of Kierkegaard in terms of the claim that Kierkegaard was fundamentally a Christian thinker. But rather than flesh this out in terms of the idea that Kierkegaard urged Christianity as a "legitimate response" to the human condition, I think it is more apt to say that Swenson sees Kierkegaard's philosophy *as fundamentally an attempt to articulate Christianity in philosophical terms*, which is not to say that he didn't also take Christianity to be a legitimate response to the human condition.

We see this point stated forcefully in the following key passage in Swenson's *Something about Kierkegaard*:

> The ultimate significance of Kierkegaard's thought and life, the place which a final accounting, if any such ever takes place, will give him in the world's history, depends absolutely upon the fate of Christianity—ultimately he stands or falls with this great world force. Its cause was the cause for which he unremittingly gave all the powers of his life, and he himself believed that he had succeeded in the task he had set for himself: *to clothe the Christian religion in the garb of philosophical reflection, complete and entire, without modification or distortion.*[16]

Worth noting is that in characterizing Kierkegaard as fundamentally a Christian philosopher, Swenson is assuming that Christianity be understood in roughly the same way as Martin Luther understood it. This point is often left as an unstated assumption in Swenson's work, but in some passages it comes up to the surface in explicit fashion. In his introduction to Eduard Geismar's *Lectures on the Religious Thought of Sören Kierkegaard* (1937), for example, he takes Kierkegaard's doctrine of Christianity as the absolute paradox to concur with "the entire spirit and purport of the personally assimilated religion which was so characteristic of Luther," adding that this is also "the central theme of Christianity."[17] Christianity was accordingly understood along Lutheran lines: Kierkegaard's Christianity is Luther's Christianity.

In sum: Swenson views Kierkegaard's philosophy as fundamentally an attempt to express Christianity philosophically. Since this is also a central characteristic of Holmer's Kierkegaard interpretation, Holmer's characterization of his interpretation as "Swensonian" appears justified.

III. The Uppsalian Background

There is more than just the Swensonian component in Holmer's Kierkegaard interpretation, however. Swenson was well aware of a group of pioneering Kierkegaard scholars, based at Uppsala in Sweden, who had been championing a "Christian" interpretation of Kierkegaard much like his own.[18] Indeed, Holmer himself cites these scholars frequently.[19]

This group of Kierkegaard scholars had two leading figures, Waldemar Rudin (1833–1921), the pioneer, and Torsten Bohlin (1889–1950), the great systematician (referred to as "the brilliant Swedish scholar" by Holmer).[20]

The controversies surrounding Kierkegaard's "attack on Christendom" in the 1850s were followed also by an audience up in Sweden. The young Rudin had taken a strong interest in these controversies during his student days at Uppsala in the 1850s.

After Kierkegaard's death in 1855, this interest was deepened by extensive studies of Kierkegaard's published writings. In the 1870s Rudin emerged as one of Sweden's foremost theologians of his time, and was appointed Professor of Theology at Uppsala, arguably the most influential theological positions anywhere in Sweden at the time.

In 1877, the year before his professorial appointment, Uppsala was visited by the Danish-Jewish literary critic and freethinker Georg Brandes, who delivered a series of lectures on Kierkegaard. In these lectures, subsequently published as *Sören Kierkegaard* (1877) and today recognized as having pioneered the field of Kierkegaard Studies,[21] Brandes praises Kierkegaard's literary talent, but complains that Kierkegaard used his gifts not in the service of "freedom" but in that of "uncritical adoration,"[22] by which he meant Christianity. Brandes sought to mitigate this aspect of Kierkegaard's thought by viewing it as the product of Kierkegaard's upbringing, family circumstances, etc., things that Kierkegaard had no power over. The proper thing to do to appreciate Kierkegaard's genius, then, was to divest it of these circumstantial religious "add-ons."

Rudin found Brandes's approach to Kierkegaard misguided, and sought to correct it by publishing his own study, *Søren Kierkegaard's Personality and Authorship* (Swe. *Sören Kierkegaards person och författarskap*) (1880).[23] In this book, Rudin claims that Brandes has gotten Kierkegaard "fundamentally wrong."[24]

He points out two basic flaws in Brandes's approach. First, that Brandes "wants to make Kierkegaard a product of his circumstances."[25] Against this, Rudin sets the view that Kierkegaard's religiosity was an effect of "the workings of divine grace and providence" and "the free choices of the individual."[26] And second, that Brandes fails to appreciate that "the very soul" in Kierkegaard's work is its Christian viewpoint.[27] To divest Kierkegaard of his Christian viewpoint is thus to miss the whole point.

Rudin's book contributed powerfully to an awakening of interest in Kierkegaard on the part of Swedish theologians in the late nineteenth and early twentieth centuries. In the 1910s we find reports in the Swedish press to the effect that Rudin's book has "guided the Swedish reading public into Kierkegaard's world of thought more than any other,"[28] and in a book on Rudin from 1923 we find the then immensely influential theologian Archbishop Nathan Söderblom praising Rudin's *Søren Kierkegaard's Personality and Authorship* as "the most agreeable presentation we have of the greatest writer and most powerful disciple of Christ in Scandinavia in modern times."[29]

One person to be particularly influenced by Rudin's book was the Uppsala theologian Bohlin, who in the late 1910s and 1920s published a series of widely acclaimed Kierkegaard studies, the most important being *Søren Kierkegaard's Ethics* (Swe. *Sören*

Kierkegaards etiska åskådning) (1918), *Søren Kierkegaard and Contemporary Religious Thought* (Swe. *Sören Kierkegaard och nutida religiöst tänkande*) (1919), and *Kierkegaard's Dogmatic Viewpoint in Its Historical Context* (Swe. *Kierkegaards dogmatiska åskådning i dess historiska sammanhang*) (1924).[30]

In *Søren Kierkegaard's Ethics*, Bohlin's first book, we find an explicit recognition of Rudin's basic claim that Kierkegaard was fundamentally a Christian thinker. According to Bohlin, Rudin's book is "beyond comparison the best work on Kierkegaard as a Christian person,"[31] and Bohlin explicitly sees himself as carrying on this approach, in opposition to more "secular" approaches to Kierkegaard. The secular approach that Bohlin has chiefly in mind is that of the German writer Wilhelm Bauer, whose *Die Ethik S. Kierkegaard* (1913) viewed Kierkegaard as having been concerned with developing an ethics of human autonomy in Kantian fashion, but whose successive failures to do so led him to incorporate religious elements into his ethics that didn't really belong there (and which with some scholarly effort could be removed). One strategy that Bohlin employs in order to undermine this secular interpretation consists in focusing on the different existential stages in Kierkegaard's *Either/Or*, and raising the question of what criterion Kierkegaard uses to classify the different stages. Bauer took the criterion to derive from a tension between the universal and the individual.[32] Bohlin rejects this, arguing instead that the criterion derives from Christianity.[33]

The ultimate flaw in Bauer's approach, then, is that it fails to see that Kierkegaard is urging a specifically Christian ethics.[34]

In *Søren Kierkegaard and Contemporary Religious Thought*, from the following year, Bohlin returns to the claim that Kierkegaard was fundamentally a Christian thinker, arguing now, a bit more specifically, that Kierkegaard worked within a framework of traditional Christian dogmatics. Thus Kierkegaard's understanding of Christianity as the absolute paradox is said to be rooted in the traditional doctrine of the two natures of Jesus Christ; Kierkegaard's understanding of sin is said to be rooted in the traditional doctrine of original sin[35]; and so on.

Bohlin's *Kierkegaard's Dogmatic Viewpoint in Its Historical Context*, finally, contains attempts to spell out in more detail the specifically Lutheran character of Kierkegaard's Christianity. Bohlin notes, for example, that Kierkegaard in *Concluding Unscientific Postscript* (1846) takes his emphasis on subjectivity to agree with Luther's stress of the need for a subjective appropriation of faith in his key Reformation treatise *On the Babylonian Captivity of the Church*[36]; that Kierkegaard in *Training in Christianity* (1850) is explicit in pointing out the "Lutheran" character of his emphasis on the need to be confronted with the fearful aspects of Christianity prior to receiving God's grace, mercy and love[37]; that Kierkegaard in *On My Activity as a Writer* (1851) explicitly declares that his intention was to prevent Luther from being reduced to insignificance in Christendom[38]; and so on. In view of these sorts of claims, Bohlin takes Kierkegaard to have regarded Luther as "the greatest figure in Christendom" and himself as "a disciple of Luther" concerned with "continuing Luther's Reformation."[39]

Bohlin's association of Kierkegaard with Luther is probably not disconnected from a strong interest at this time among Swedish theologians as to the life and work of Luther. Uppsala was at this time the center of a "Luther renaissance"; an enormous number of books and dissertations on various aspects of Luther's thought were being published, and there was a widespread belief that Luther represented an authentic form of personal Christianity that had stood the test of time and Western modernization.[40] In this cultural context, aligning Kierkegaard with Luther would no doubt have helped bolster Kierkegaard's image.

IV. Swenson's Distancing of Himself from Bohlin

If the roots of Holmer's Kierkegaard interpretation trace back to the Uppsalian Kierkegaard interpretation, why isn't this better known? In this concluding section, I offer some conjectures on this.

The main reason why the Uppsalian roots of Holmer's Kierkegaard interpretation aren't better known is, I believe, because Swenson did not properly acknowledge them, even to the point of occasionally situating himself *against* the Uppsalian Kierkegaard interpretation.[41] Since Holmer was a student of Swenson's, Swenson's occasional disagreement with the Uppsalians is likely to have made also Holmer less prone to cite these scholars as his own intellectual predecessors.

A reason why Swenson occasionally situated himself against the Uppsalian Kierkegaard interpretation may be as follows. Bohlin had endorsed the view of early-twentieth-century liberal theologians like Albrecht Ritschl, Adolf von Harnack, and Wilhelm Herrmann that various doctrines in traditional Christian dogmatics are neither authentically Christian nor rooted in genuine religious experience, but are instead part of an intellectual superstructure that goes back to the influence of Greek philosophy on Christian theology. Since Bohlin took Kierkegaard to work within a traditional Christian theological framework, he found reason to claim that those aspects of Kierkegaard's thought that he believed were not rooted in genuine religious experience were not authentically Christian. Accordingly, in *Søren Kierkegaard and Contemporary Religious Thought* he says that Kierkegaard's view of sin, and of Christianity as the absolute paradox, "belong to the past," inasmuch as they are based on Greek ideas about the divine as "eternal" and the human as "temporal."[42] Since Bohlin, along with most Swedish theologians at this time, took the Lutheran Reformation to have revived authentic Christianity,[43] it was concluded that the relevant aspects of Kierkegaard's thought were foreign to "an evangelical understanding of Christianity," notwithstanding Kierkegaard's basic Christian and Lutheran orientation.[44]

In the late 1930s and 1940s, and under the influence of Dialectical and Lundensian Theology (both of which were strongly theocentric), Bohlin's criticisms of Kierkegaard came under heavy attack. Major critics included Valter Lindström, another major figure in early Swedish Kierkegaard Studies, and the well-known Danish Kierkegaard scholar Aage Kabell. Lindström's objection was that Bohlin's criticisms displayed a bias toward a particular theological idea as to what constitutes authentic Christianity.[45] Kabell's objection was that Bohlin's criticisms disregarded the element of paradox in Lutheran Christianity.[46]

That Swenson was aware of Bohlin's theologically liberal criticisms of Kierkegaard is clear, for example, from his introduction to Eduard Geismar's *Lectures on the Religious Thought of Sören Kierkegaard*. He here offers a spirited defense of Kierkegaard's idea of Christianity as the absolute paradox over against Bohlin's criticisms, saying, among other things, that

> it is in order to ask him [Bohlin] whether *he* can understand how God can forgive *his* sins. If he answers "yes," he comes into sharp conflict with the entire spirit and purport of the

personally assimilated religion which was so characteristic of Luther ... And if he answers "no," he has *ipso facto* established the paradoxical as a category with respect to the central theme of Christianity.[47]

The strong emotional undertone in the above quotation is unmistakable: Swenson was deeply disturbed by the criticisms Bohlin leveled against Kierkegaard. And this, understandably, led him to take a negative view of Bohlin's work as a whole, in spite of the strong affinities and overlaps between Bohlin's work and his own.

That Swenson developed an overall negative view of Bohlin's work is rendered evident by a paper on Swenson by his former colleague C. Sverre Norborg, who relates the following incident in 1937:

> I well remember one morning in the early spring of 1937 when we stood in our office discussing the Danish philosopher. In the course of the conversation I happened to mention the two compact volumes by the Swedish scholar Torsten Bohlin. Immediately a Socratic smile passed over Swenson's face. "Bohlin! Ah, but that man never understood Kierkegaard's fundamental intention. He has made a 'system' out of Kierkegaard, very much in the same manner as a scientist pinning his dead butterflies. But Kierkegaard is a

subjective thinker who insists that the existential can never be systematized."[48]

Swenson here dismisses Bohlin as having "never understood" Kierkegaard's "fundamental intention." This is a strange claim to make of a scholar who concurred with him in regarding Kierkegaard as fundamentally a Lutheran Christian thinker. Nevertheless, if we take into account that Swenson's evaluation of Bohlin was impacted by a deep-rooted antipathy toward Bohlin's criticisms of Kierkegaard, it is understandable that he would have made such a dismissive claim.

V. In Conclusion

It appears that Swenson's theologically motivated antipathy toward Bohlin served to cloud the extent to which his interpretation of Kierkegaard, and indirectly also Holmer's, was indebted to the Uppsalian Kierkegaard interpretation going back to Rudin and Bohlin. This indebtedness implies that the Religious Interpretation of Kierkegaard in North American Kierkegaard scholarship famously associated with Swenson's student Holmer, indirectly traces back to the Uppsalian Kierkegaard interpretation, which in turn was a direct negative reaction to Brandes's attempt to secularize Kierkegaard by turning the religious philosopher par excellence into a sort of literary genius with an accidental religious hangover from childhood.

Notes

1 Paul L. Holmer, "Kierkegaard and Theology" (1957), reprinted in Holmer: *Thinking the Faith with Passion*, ed. David Gouwens and Lee C. Barrett III (Eugene, OR: Cascade Books, 2012), pp. 42–52, at p. 42. (Originally published in *Union Seminary Quarterly Review*.)

2 Holmer, *On Kierkegaard and the Truth*, p. xvi, 52, 110. Holmer usually contrasts this "Christian" interpretation of Kierkegaard with Ernst Cassirer's view that Kierkegaard was an "unbeliever"; see, for example, *On Kierkegaard and the Truth*, p. 22, and *Kierkegaard and the Truth*, p. 10. (Holmer doesn't refer to any passage in Cassirer's writings where this claim is made. Cassirer had been Holmer's teacher at Yale in the early 1940s, so it is possible that the claim was made verbally.)

3 See Kierkegaard, *Either/Or*, vol. 2, trans. Howard and Edna Hong (Princeton: Princeton University Press, 1987), pp. 335–54.

4 Kierkegaard, *Either/Or*, vol. 2, p. 354.

5 See Kierkegaard, "Concluding Unscientific Postscript," in *A Kierkegaard Anthology*, ed. Robert Bretall (New York: The Modern Library, 1946), pp. 210–26.

6 Holmer, *Kierkegaard and the Truth*, p. 1 (my emphasis).

7 Holmer, *Kierkegaard and the Truth*, pp. 270–1 (my emphasis).

8 Paul L. Holmer, *On Kierkegaard and the Truth*, ed. David Gouwens and Lee C. Barrett III (Eugene, OR: Cascade Books, 2012), p. xxvi.

9 Paul L. Holmer, *Kierkegaard and the Truth: An Analysis of the Presuppositions Integral to His Definition of Truth* (New Haven: Yale University, Ph.D. dissertation, 1946), p. iii.

10 The episode is narrated by Swenson in *Something about Kierkegaard*, pp. 1–2. Mary Carmen Rose, and more recently David Gouwens and Lee C. Barrett III, date the episode to 1898, but George P. Conger dates the episode to 1901; see, respectively, Mary Carmen Rose, "Swenson on Kierkegaard," in David F. Swenson: *Something about Kierkegaard*, ed. Lillian M. Swenson (Macon, GA: Mercer University Press, 2003), p. vii; Paul L. Holmer, *On Kierkegaard and the Truth*, ed. David Gouwens and Lee C. Barrett III (Eugene, OR: Cascade Books, 2012), pp. xv–xxii, at p. xvi; and George P. Conger, "David F. Swenson as a Teacher and a Personality," in *David F. Swenson: Scholar, Teacher, Friend*, ed. George P. Conger (Minneapolis: Lund Press, 1940), p. 9. The episode is of historical significance as it may be said to mark the beginning of Kierkegaard Studies in America.

11 Cf. Rose, "Swenson on Kierkegaard," pp. vii–viii.

12 See Conger, "David F. Swenson as a Teacher and a Personality," pp. 7–12, at p. 7.

13 David F. Swenson: *Something about Kierkegaard*, ed. Lillian M. Swenson (Macon, GA: Mercer University Press, 2003), pp. xii–xxiv, at p. xiv.

14 Conger, "David F. Swenson as a Teacher and a Personality," p. 9.

15 Gouwens and Barrett III, "Editors' Preface," pp. xv–xxii, at p. xvii.

16 Swenson, *Something about Kierkegaard*, pp. 25–6 (my emphasis). See also Swenson's remark that "[t]he entire Kierkegaardian literature ... describes the movement in reflection so that the author reflects himself out of everything else, the esthetic, the poetic, the philosophical—in order to become the simple, straightforward, plain uninteresting, moral personality—a Christian"; *Something about Kierkegaard*, 65.

17 David F. Swenson, "Editor's Introduction," in Eduard Geismar: *Lectures on the Religious Thought of Sören Kierkegaard* (Minneapolis: Augsburg Publishing House, 1937), pp. iii–xxx, at p. xxvii.

18 See, e.g., Swenson's remark in 1935 that "It may be of importance to mention that both Bohlin and Geismar indirectly support my interpretation of the Paradox-idea [in Kierkegaard]"; see his "Letter

to Dr. Lowrie" (September 14, 1935), in *Something about Kierkegaard*, 218–22, 221.

19 See, e.g., Holmer, *Kierkegaard and the Truth*, p. 163, 213, 256, 293; *On Kierkegaard and the Truth*, p. 44; cf. 63.

20 Holmer, *On Kierkegaard and the Truth*, p. 44; cf. 63.

21 George Brandes, *Sören Kierkegaard* (Stockholm: Seligmann, 1877). The book was published simultaneously in Danish as *Søren Kierkegaard. En kritisk fremstilling i grundrids* (Kjøbenhavn: Gyldendal, 1877), reprinted in Georg Brandes, *Samlede Skrifter*, vol. 2 (Kjøbenhavn: Gyldendalske Boghandels forlag, 1899), pp. 249–418.

22 Brandes: *Samlede Skrifter*, p. 260, 262. (My translation.)

23 Waldemar Rudin, *Sören Kierkegaards person och författarskap: Ett försök* (Stockholm: A. Nilsson, 1880). (All translations from Rudin's original Swedish into English are my own.)

24 Ibid., p. 4.

25 Ibid., p. 5.

26 Ibid., p. 5.

27 Ibid., p. 4.

28 F. Dahlbom, "Torsten Bohlin: Sören Kierkegaards etiska åskådning; med särskild hänsyn till begreppet 'den enskilde,'" *Svensk kyrkotidning*, vol. 14 (1918), p. 439. (My translation.)

29 Nathan Söderblom, *Waldemar Rudins inre liv* (Stockholm: Norstedt, 1923), p. 78. (My translation.)

30 For discussions of some of these studies and the historical context in which they were written, see my "Bohlin, Torsten: *Sören Kierkegaards etiska åskådning*" and Anders Kraal, "Bohlin, Torsten: Sören Kierkegaards etiska åskådning," and Anders Kraal, "Bohlin, Torsten: Sören Kierkegaard och nutida religiöst tänkande," in Kierkegaard Secondary Literature, tome 6, ed. Jon Stewart (Aldershot: Ashgate, 2017), 253–6, and 256–66.

31 Torsten Bohlin, *Sören Kierkegaards etiska åskådning. Med särskild hänsyn till begreppet "den enskilde"* (Stockholm: Svenska kyrkans diakonistyrelses bokförlag, 1918), p. v. (All translations from Bohlin's original Swedish into English are my own.)

32 Ibid., pp. 120–4.

33 Ibid., pp. 113–19.

34 Ibid., p. 124.

35 Ibid., pp. 94–5, 80.

36 Bohlin, *Kierkegaards dogmatiska åskådning i dess historiska sammanhang* (Stockholm: Svenska Kyrkans Diakonistyrelses Bokförlag 1925), p. 445. For the relevant passage in Kierkegaard, see *Afsluttende uvidenskabelig Efterskrift* (1846), in *Søren Kierkegaards Skrifter*, ed. Niels Jørgen Cappelørn, Joakim Garff, Johnny Kondrup, Karsten Kynde, Tonny Aagaard Olesen and Steen Tullberg (Copenhagen: Søren Kierkegaard Forskningscenteret, 2014), vol. 7, pp. 332–3.

37 Bohlin, *Kierkegaards dogmatiska åskådning i dess historiska sammanhang*, pp. 445–6. For the relevant passage in Kierkegaard, see Kierkegaard, *Indøvelse i Christendom* (1850), in *Søren Kierkegaards Skrifter*, vol. 12, pp. 79–80.

38 Ibid., p. 442.

39 Ibid., p. 441.

40 For an overview of the Luther Renaissance in Swedish theology during the first few decades of the twentieth century, see Anders Kraal, "Free Choice, Determinism, and the Re-evaluation of Luther in Twentieth-Century Swedish Theology," *Studia Theologica*, 67:1 (2013), pp. 28–42.

41 See, e.g., *David F. Swenson: Scholar, Teacher, Friend*, ed. George P. Conger (Minneapolis: Lund Press, 1940), pp. 14–24, at p. 14.

42 Bohlin, *Sören Kierkegaards etiska åskådning*, pp. 68–9, 130. These criticisms are repeated also in Bohlin's last major Kierkegaard study, *Sören Kierkegaard: Mannen och verket* [Sören Kierkegaard: The

Man and His Work] (Stockholm: Svenska kyrkans diakonistyrelses bokförlag, 1939), pp. 292–3.

43 For more on this, see my "Free Choice, Determinism, and the Reevaluation of Luther in Twentieth Century Swedish Theology," *Studia theologica* 67 (2013), pp. 28–42.

44 Bohlin, *Sören Kierkegaards etiska åskådning*, p. 130.

45 See Valter Lindström, "Torsten Bohlin: Sören Kierkegaard. Mannen och verket. 322 sid. Svenska kyrkans diakonistyrelses bokförlag, Stockholm (tr. i Uppsala) 1939. Pris kr. 7:50, inb. Kr. 9:50," *Svensk Teologisk Kvartalskrift*, vol. 17 (1941), p. 71; *Stadiernas teologi: En Kierkegaardstudie* (Lund: C.W.K. Gleerup, 1943), pp. 10–11; and *Efterföljelsens teologi hos Sören Kierkegaard* (Stockholm: Svenska kyrkans diakonistyrelses bokförlag, 1956), p. 44. For an overview of the Bohlin-Lindström debate, see Aage Henriksen, *Kierkegaard Studies in Scandinavia: A Historical and Critical Survey* (Copenhagen: Ejnar Munksgaard, 1951), pp. 141–58.

46 Aage Kabell, *Kierkegaardstudiet i Norden* (Copenhagen: H. Hagerup, 1948), p. 178.

47 Swenson, "Editor's Introduction," p. xxvii.

48 Norberg, "David F. Swenson as a Scholar," p. 14.

4
Paul Holmer and the Logic of Preaching
Jeffrey Willetts

Holmer at YDS

From 1960 to 1987, Paul Holmer was the Noah Porter Professor of Philosophical Theology at Yale Divinity School (YDS). From 1985 to 1987, I had the good fortune to take four courses in philosophical theology with Holmer toward a Master of Arts in Religion: "Readings in Kierkegaard"; "Wittgenstein and Meaning"; "Devotion and Theology"; and "Philosophical Theology."

Holmer's courses were always thoroughly philosophical in character; but not in the manner so often associated with twentieth-century Anglo-American philosophy. In fact Holmer's philosophical approach operated as a kind of counter-movement in thought against many of the philosophical and theological trends of his day. His work functioned as a kind of check against any and all theological system building, the intellectually attractive but unwarranted appropriation of various philosophies for theology, and the tendency in theology to abstract the meaning of theological language in terms external to the Christian life. In this respect, Holmer was more sage than scientist, more disarming prophet than mediating priest, and as such, his role in the Divinity school, at least in the latter part of his career, was experienced by many as—Socratic gadfly.

In the 1980s, YDS was populated with many trend-setting figures in the various theological disciplines: Brevard Childs—canonical theology, Letty Russell—feminist theology, George Lindbeck and David Kelsey—post-liberal theology, along with Hans Frei down the hill. Others would become trend-setters latter on, such as Richard Hays in New Testament ethics or Cornell West in black theology and social justice theory.

Holmer was no trend setter. In fact, his entire intellectual orientation mitigated against it. As a consequence, Holmer was seemingly so far out of the theological mainstream, his place within the school's intellectual constellation was sometimes uncertain in the eyes of some students and colleagues. On one occasion, near the end of term, Brevard Childs invited his upper-level Biblical Theology students over to his home. In the course of the conversation, attention turned to each student's intellectual interests. My interests were firmly rooted in Wittgenstein and

Kierkegaard, and I expressed my appreciation for Professor Holmer's contribution to those interests. Professor Childs, recognizing my regard for Holmer's intellectual perspective, responded with a gentlemanly retort, "Well, we've never known quite what to do with Paul."

In his role as gadfly, Holmer's sense of humor and wry wit were experienced by students and colleagues alike as disarming, abrupt, and for some even harsh. Others found him amusing, personally engaging, and even humorous. But his brief asides and caustic commentary always had a point. One always had the sense that his irony laced remarks were more, moments of exceptional clarity, rather than bald criticism—breaking through the "chatter" and "noise" of all kinds of theory-making and intellectual enthusiasms; leaving one with the distinct impression that he had seen down to the very bottom of things, while rest of us lived with dim reflections and shadowy appearances.

On another occasion, while crossing the Quad, I happened to pass Professor Holmer on my way to the cafeteria. He asked me how it was going, and I told him about my internship as a teaching assistant in ethics at one of the local universities. He thought that was fine, but in the course of our brief conversation I expressed my surprise concerning the supervising ethics professor's approach to the subject: "She has the idea that all moral convictions are based on some deeper ethical theory," to which Holmer replied, "Yeah, with her I would want to start way back."

In a similar vein, an apocryphal story circulating at that time recounted a Common Room event (the Common Room at YDS was often the location for the community to have a public discussion of some relevant theological topic) in which the historicity of the Bible was the advertised topic for discussion. Because Holmer was the anticipated respondent, the event drew a larger than usual crowd. As the presenter concluded his remarks, the moment turned to Holmer's rebuttal. As he began, he looked out over the group and said, *"you all look like you are here to join a cause. Well, Christianity isn't a cause!"*

This kind of jarring rhetoric was typical of Holmer and it had the effect sometimes of causing offense, sometimes confusion, but always pause, for the sake of deeper reflection. Indeed, sometimes his remarks were so penetrating they occasioned the reordering of one's outlook on a particular theological problem or led one in an entirely different intellectual direction. In this case, it was classic Holmer; one well-placed remark, challenging students to consider the "how" of their Christian lives, thereby clarifying the "what" of their energies and efforts.

Holmer's Influence

This is not to say that Holmer's role at that time was always perceived as ambiguous or negative by his colleagues. Indeed, his influence went deep and he was not without his allies. In the fall of 1985, the Welsh philosopher, DZ Phillips, a leading interpreter of Wittgenstein for the philosophy of religion, was a Visiting scholar at Yale.[1] During that semester, Phillips taught one course in philosophy of religion titled, "Dubious Dualisms" and wrote the first half of his book, *Faith after Foundationalism*.[2] In that work, Phillips takes up critically the work of a number of figures at YDS at the time, including George Lindbeck, Cornell West, and Holmer himself.

At a Common Room event that term, Phillips presented a paper he titled, "Lindbeck's Audience."[3] In his remarks Phillips challenged various philosophical suppositions integral to Lindbeck's theological methodology in his *The Nature of Doctrine*.[4] After a forty-minute critical assessment of Lindbeck's work, Lindbeck simply thanked Phillips for his remarks and concluded the event without a response, bringing the occasion to an odd and abrupt halt.

The interaction was not so one-sided later that term when students gathered at Holmer's home for a second presentation by Phillips, his paper titled "Holmer's Audience."[5] Again, because Holmer was the advertised respondent, the occasion was highly anticipated. Holmer was as formidable on this occasion as Phillips, and the mutual respect between them was evident. Indeed, of all the philosophers and theologians Phillips criticizes in his *Faith after Foundationalism*, Holmer receives the most sympathetic reading. "Holmer's Audience," Phillips says, "was a reaction to Paul Holmer's *The Grammar of Faith*[6] which I already knew and had found philosophically congenial."[7]

Phillips' reaction to Holmer marked Holmer's considerable influence. Though Holmer was sometimes enigmatic to his colleagues, and though he did not publish a great deal during his life-time, that did not mean he did not have a profound impact on the YDS community, or the contemporary theological landscape more broadly. As Mark Horst notes, shortly after Holmer's retirement in 1988, "Many of his colleagues, including Brevard Childs, whose work in Old Testament studies has helped chart a new agenda for biblical studies in this country, and George Lindbeck, whose seminal work in theological methodology has attracted so much attention recently, owe a debt to Holmer."[8] Indeed, both Sydney Ahlstrom and George Lindbeck were Holmer's students at Adolphus Gustavo College where Holmer taught before he came to Yale in 1960. And while at YDS Holmer influenced an entire generation of notable philosophers, theologians, and ministers, including Stanley Hauerwas, Don Saliers, Richard H. Bell, Sylvia Walsh, Robert C. Roberts, John H. Whittaker, William Willimon, and many others. And of course, he influenced hundreds and hundreds of less notable but no less important future preachers and religious teachers who passed through the halls of YDS throughout his twenty-seven-year career there.

Beyond Holmer's direct influence on colleagues and students, he also had a bearing on theology more widely in North America. As the editors of *Holmer's Papers* have rightly indicated, his "reflections were *sui generis* ... and he had a pervasive and significant (but often unacknowledged) impact upon the development of Christian reflection in the United States in the second half of the twentieth century."[9] His influence was subtle, and his criticisms were mostly outside the mainstream, but for those who encountered his thought, the result of Holmer's influence was occasion for serious revision to one's thought, sometimes the complete abandonment of certain ways of thinking, or as Stanley Hauerwas has it—life changing—"How Paul Holmer ruined my life."[10]

Holmer's Approach

At the core of Holmer's philosophical approach to theology was a powerful and impressive appreciation and application of the seminal insights of both Kierkegaard and Wittgenstein. As Richard Bell summarizes in his *festschrift* for Holmer, he

> began to wed some of the ideas of Kierkegaard and Wittgenstein in ways that gave new liveliness to their works and suggested some new directions in which moral philosophy

and theology might develop. No longer was Kierkegaard just an "existentialist" thinker, nor could Wittgenstein be constrained within narrow "analytic" bounds."[11]

What made Holmer's particular way of engaging the philosophical and theological guilds so impressive was the clarity with which he blended the insights of Kierkegaard and Wittgenstein to produce a truly comprehensive critique of contemporary philosophical and theological approaches to religious language. For Holmer, those approaches are typically marked by a tendency to import alien paradigms of meaning to the understanding of religious language, and by so doing, distorting the very meaning of the theological concepts the philosophical and theological analysis was meant to clarify. Methodologically, Holmer offers what Holmer himself describes as "a morphology of the life of Christian belief, a logic and a grammar that we miss often because a monstrous illusion is fostered by a pattern of thought and speech, wherein objectivity, fact, meaning, truth, and even faith are advertised but never delivered."[12] At the core of that critique was an insight into the nature of religious language that saw a radical logical distinction between understanding religious beliefs in the *about* mode as opposed to the *of* mode. To that end, Holmer rightly insists "that there can be no generic theory of meaning by which we can say that scientific language is more meaningful than religious language."

In fact, the whole notion of meaning is itself confused and it might be better simply to say that we can learn the differences between ways of speaking and ways of understanding …. One way to express this fully is to declare that the logic of the discourse of science is not the same as the logic of religion. Another way is to note all the different ways that we explain things to ourselves. For again there are many kinds of explanation. Each kind has its context, its occasion, its own province, and its own function, relative to a specific need. We are gradually learning that kinds of explanations are not necessarily incompatible. They are in fact incommensurable with one another, and hence there is no logical incompatibility of the radical sort.[13]

Holmer's Audience

D.Z. Phillips highlights this feature of Holmer's contribution to philosophy in so far as Holmer's philosophical approach to theology demonstrates how approaches that "stand in external relation to a living faith," or in the *about* mode in respect of religious language are distortions rooted in a common confusion.[14] In his paper titled "Grammarians and Guardians,"[15] Phillips recognizes four different groups of theologians he identifies as "Holmer's Audience." Each of these groups in one way or another appeals to an external relation between religious language and its meaning.

The first group of theologians whom Holmer is said to address, according to Phillips, is those "theologians who think that implicit in the living faith is the philosophical foundation of it. The foundation is called *theism*."[16] According to Holmer, there is something absurd about this. "Crucifying Jesus, living faithlessly, and loving the world with all one's heart, soul, mind and strength tend then to become trivialities compared with denying theism. It is almost as if the academies have made crucial what was not so initially."[17] One might argue that seeing *theism* as the crucial rational foundation of theological language is a form of conceptual dislocation, the result of which is to leave the ordinary language of faith as a tertiary matter. Indeed, the rationality of the great Abrahamic faiths is said to depend on the demonstration of certain metaphysical truths; thus the importance of the traditional proofs to the practice of theology.

But of course, the traditional proofs, as Phillips reminds us, inevitably encounter insuperable difficulties. If we acknowledge the confusion that the proofs bring as a form of external justification of a living faith, "we can see that concepts at work in a living Faith do not derive their meaning and vitality from the abstract concepts of theism. On the contrary, whatever life theism ever had in it was derived from the special, but ordinary concepts of a working Faith."[18]

The second group of theologians Holmer is said to address is those theologians who think that faith is rationally dependent upon *historical kinds of knowledge*; that in order for something to be true it must be answerable to the *facts*. As Phillips summarizes, "Holmer is worried at signs of many settling for historical knowledge as if it were an adequate substitute for theology. There is a desperate confusion in the assumption that such a substitution makes sense."[19] But coming to know certain historical truths does not have the same logical or grammatical character as coming to know certain religious truths. According to Holmer:

> it is far more important than most historical material to learn to hunger and thirst for righteousness, to learn to love a neighbor, and to achieve a high degree of self-concern, in order to understand the religious themes of the New Testament. There are, in short, personality qualifications that are also required. Perhaps it is even essential to have learned guilt because one has not done as he ought to have done. In any case, these forms of human consciousness are closer to the prerequisites for a Christian understanding than is most knowledge supplied by other scholars.[20]

The third group of theologians Holmer is said to address is those theologians for whom historical facts are conceptually unsatisfactory. There is the tendency among liberal theologians, Phillips suggests, to want to talk about, not historical facts, as such, but *religious facts* instead. When one is convinced that the truths of religion cannot be ascertained by historical investigation, one may be tempted to create a conception of a different kind of history, a *religious history*, which has to do with *special facts*—religious facts upon which the truths of one's religious beliefs and practice depend. Or, alternatively, conservative theologians, not trusting *special facts* of religious history, will reassert their commitment to the facts, as we have them from the faith itself: the authority of the Scriptures, for example, or the teaching of the church—somehow guaranteeing their truth. In either case, those whose appeal to a *special set of facts*, i.e., the content of a religious history, or those who appeal to the authority of the Bible or the tradition as its special guarantee, leads inexorably to accounts of the meaning of religious language that leave the very grammar or logic of that language unaccounted for.[21]

The fourth group of theologians Holmer is said to address are those theologians who having wearied of, or reacted against, the theologians noted above, argue for the foundational importance of religious experience, "a religious experience without theology." According to Phillips, Holmer is sympathetic to the reactions of these theologians, but ***not*** [my emphasis] with the implications they draw from them. Despair at confused theologies should not lead on to jettison theology altogether. Experience without the governance of theology is wild and undisciplined. Furthermore, turning away from the concepts of the Christian Faith towards experience is to misunderstand the role of these concepts.[22]

Indeed, to appropriate theological concepts is to learn the authorization for "all kinds of dispositions, feelings, passions, virtues and deeds that make one's daily living something distinctive. They even produce another view of the world and human life."[23] Therefore, for Holmer, to grasp a theological concept is to develop a capacity.

One way in which to understand what Holmer is commending to his audience is to explore more specifically how the appropriation of theological concepts and thereby certain capacities is supposed to happen. Not only did Holmer recognize and contend with various kinds of conceptual confusion in theology; he was ever interested in *trying to make sense* of the Christian faith, as such. As the recent publication of his unpublished works makes clear, a great deal of Holmer's intellectual output was a conceptual exploration of and reflection on various Christian practices: baptism, marriage, worship, liturgy, the celebration of the Christian calendar, such as Advent, Christian living, etc. Preaching and teaching were important to Holmer, as his many essays, lectures, and occasioned remarks suggest.[24] And, for Holmer, preaching had a particularly significant role to play.

Preaching Is a Venturesome Thing ...

In an essay published in 1971, Holmer etches for his audience a picture of the way in which the language of faith, and more particularly the logic or grammar of preaching operates within the Christian faith: "Indirect Communication: Something about the Sermon (With References to Kierkegaard and Wittgenstein)."[25]

In the Preface to the collection in which this essay has recently reappeared, the editors remind us that "For Holmer, the challenge but also the glory of the sermon or religious address is to communicate not so much the 'language *about* faith' but the 'language *of* faith.'"[26] In an interview in 1988, Holmer argues for the interrelated character of theology with preaching,

> My teeth have been put on edge both in the church and the seminaries. And they've stayed on edge ... as if preaching is something independent of theology and as if preaching is optional and only certain people do that, whereas I would

think that having the words of faith on your lips is one of the ways to be a Christian.[27]

In this essay, with Kierkegaard and Wittgenstein very much in the foreground, Holmer undertakes to lead his listeners (in its original presentation) and readers into a new appreciation of the logically distinctive *kind of thing* that is Christian preaching. According to Willimon,

Holmer insists that the sermon or religious address is in no wise inferior to formal theology, the latter often falsely thought to be the "real understanding." Rather, the sermon is itself the understanding of the Christian faith, insofar as it displays the "logic" of Christian faith, showing the shape of Christian faith not only in its beliefs, but in the way that it shapes our human capacities and challenges too our "emotions, passions, and feelings."[28]

To this end, Holmer invites us to view the question of the logic of preaching through the lens of Soren Kierkegaard's arresting remark, ***preaching is a venturesome thing.***

What the Sermon Is Not ...

In *Section I* of his essay "Indirect Communication: Something about the Sermon (With References to Kierkegaard and

Wittgenstein)," Holmer explores the sense of the sermon; the logic, if you will, of preaching; the something that separates preaching from all other forms of speech or discourse; and he does so by pondering Kierkegaard's notion that *preaching is a venturesome thing.*

For Holmer, making sense of this form of Christian discourse is firstly to recognize *what preaching is not*. Preaching, for example, is not simply a form of "chatter," words strung together such that when one has ceased to speak, there it is—a sermon. Nor is it a crafty or clever use of words, expressed in such a way as to stimulate others to action, or to tears, or some deep feeling or emotion. Nor is preaching a kind of performance by which one speaks and is successful if one gets "something originally said by another appropriately transmitted."[29] These are obvious ways in which, for Holmer, speaking *is not preaching*. The point, seemingly trivial, is that all *speaking* is **not** *preaching*. Why? Because these forms of speaking are not venturesome, and preaching, if Kierkegaard is right, is a *venturesome thing*.

Venturesome Preaching ...

But, then, in what sense *is* preaching *venturesome*? Holmer pursues this question by exploring multiple contexts highlighted by Kierkegaard within which it would make sense to characterize this venerable Christian practice as *venturesome*.[30]

It is venturesome to preach, for example, in front of large audiences, and speak to people one does not know. This form of speech is clearly venturesome and fairly common place. But its venturesome character is limited. In this case, it is likely, over time, that one learns what it is to speak in front of others, particularly persons one does not know. It is also likely that over time one grows accustomed to large audiences. Once one learns the kinds of techniques that assist one in speaking before others, the trepidation and anxiety that accompany public speaking soon evaporate and the venturesome character of speaking/preaching is no longer venturesome and therefore no longer distinguishable from other forms of speaking in other contexts.[31]

It is venturesome to preach on topics about which one may be insufficiently knowledgeable. This form of venturesomeness in preaching is not hard to imagine if one considers the immensity of the potential topics about which one must speak: God, Creation, the World, the Christian life, etc. The magnitude of each topic, according to Holmer, would naturally yield a kind of reticence or diffidence. And there are the inherent difficulties attendant in saying something about a being whom the scriptures tell us is unsearchable and the theologians tell us is invisible and ineffable. And that is not to mention all the special skills one may need to master, such as reading Hebrew and Greek, in order to be sure one's exposition of the scriptures for the purposes of preaching is sound.[32]

It is venturesome to preach if what one must say is against the weight of the evidence. That is, the kind declaration one may make in the course of preaching may have the character of venturing beyond the probabilities. In a sense one places one's credibility on the line in advancing notions for which the jury is clearly still out.[33]

Preaching may also be venturesome, if what one has to say is against the political tide, or is aimed at the powers that be, or is in the interest of justice and "in a world of compromise and complacency, might indeed be dangerous." History demonstrates rather conclusively that the majority do not want to hear the truth and in this respect, to preach is indeed a venturesome thing.[34]

So for all the reasons Holmer outlines above, it is obvious that preaching may indeed be a venturesome thing. But, do such examples fit the *venturesomeness* identified by Kierkegaard's arresting remark. Holmer argues, no. Although Kierkegaard would not deny that the venturesome forms and occasions of speech enumerated above are *kinds of venturesomeness* in preaching, they do not represent the radical character of what Holmer takes Kierkegaard to be elucidating in his remark, *preaching is a venturesome thing*. According to Holmer:

> what he [Kierkegaard] had noticed about these matters seemed to him to invite more than circumstantial remarks,

something different from observations on the particularities of preaching granted the pastor's immaturity, his relative ignorance, his idealism, his moral enthusiasms, and the faults of the present generation.[35]

In the examples of *venturesomeness* above, the venturesome character of preaching is largely circumstantial. The venturesome character of the sermon is externally related to the circumstances of the sermon itself. The venturesomeness of the preaching is not necessary to the subjectivity of either the hearer or the speaker. To think of the sermon in the manner characterized above would leave the hearer to understand the point or lesson or meaning of the sermon in the *about* mode, and connecting to the speaker in an contingent and external relation. And that is precisely where and how the force of Kierkegaard's remark, that *preaching is a venturesome thing*, is lost. If preaching is theology and theology is preaching, and theology is best done, properly done, only rightly done, **not** in the *about* mode, but in a manner that is logically internal to the life of the hearer and speaker, then sermons, properly understood, are venturesome in some far more radical way. Says Holmer, "Sermons, therefore, are not aiming to cover the *subject (emphasis mine)* of faith. So it is wrong to suggest a sermon tells one *what* Christianity is in a direct and ordinary way, almost as an answer to the question, what is it anyway? There is no telling in quite that way."[36] Rather, the sermon is connected to what in Kierkegaard is the very focus of his writing which is *how one becomes a Christian*. It is in *this* respect that Holmer wants to argue that the sermon, the act of preaching *is a venturesome thing*.

Venturesome Preaching ...

So what is preaching with respect to how one becomes a Christian and in what sense does that dimension of preaching make it venturesome? In order to make sense of this logical dynamic, Holmer outlines the long path by which Kierkegaard arrives at his conclusions.

Holmer notes that early on Kierkegaard was a student of Aristotle's *The Art of Rhetoric*. What Kierkegaard saw in Aristotle's reflections on rhetoric were linguistic distinctions that identified specific kinds of speech: dramatic speech, persuasive speech, pedagogical speech, etc., each with discernible rules that could be articulated. Because in Kierkegaard's day, it was philosophically fashionable to believe that language and words had meanings irrespective of their time and place, Aristotle's commentary on speech worked for Kierkegaard as a kind of counter point to a generalizing philosophical spirit that minimized attention to the context and use of words and language. *Differences*, rather than commonalities, in the use of language is what began to loom large for Kierkegaard, which begins to shape what would emerge as Kierkegaard's understanding and deployment of the notion of *indirect communication*.

Holmer asks:

What about the sermon? Was it to be subsumed under Aristotle's categories as one more instance of persuasion, or did it need a closer look and better characterization? It was surely the latter. And this is how those striking things about "indirect communication" can be understood. That expression is designed to make one see the differences between lecturing and preaching, ordinary talking and preaching, even between a bit of reflective prose and a homily (either moral or religious). And that remark, "indirect communication," is very much in the manner of what Wittgenstein called a grammatical remark. It forced one to think about the way a sermon hung together, how it worked and just what the aims and purposes, therefore, could be. Neither a general philosophy of language, even if it included a theory about how every word "meant," nor a commodious scheme of kinds of rhetoric would quite do the job of showing one the differences that made a sermon.[37]

Indirect Communication and Venturesome Preaching

In *Section II* of his lecture, Holmer, with reference to Wittgenstein, sets out to characterize the sense in which for Kierkegaard, preaching operates as a form of *indirect communication*. Holmer begins with the early Wittgenstein and his notion of the unutterable, "things that cannot be put into words." For the early Wittgenstein, much of what is important cannot be said, they must be shown, "They make themselves manifest."[38] According to Holmer, "here, of course, he is talking about very confounding matters, about 'the problem of life,' apparently also the sense of life, about what makes for the differences between the world of the happy man and that of the unhappy man."[39]

Holmer sees in the early Wittgenstein an affinity with Kierkegaard's early struggle to escape the generalizing logic of Hegel and his followers. Kierkegaard believed Hegelian philosophy had disastrously distorted the character of Christian believing. In order to escape the "monstrous illusion" Kierkegaard had to move his audience in a new direction.

> He, therefore, had to think in a new and cryptic way about words, concepts, logic, reality questions. He described that odyssey variously as out of the complexity, into the simple;

out of the aesthetic, through the ethical, into the religious; out of the manifold, through the philosophical, into the simple again.[40]

So also in Wittgenstein, according to Holmer, "there is at least something that goes on in the reader of Wittgenstein that reminds one of the effect of Kierkegaard. He makes one see differences. He does not lump things and then believe that you have understood."

In this respect, Holmer recognizes what is of particular significance in Wittgenstein's early logical distinction between *saying* and *showing*.

Wittgenstein thought that language sometimes showed you something that strictly speaking was not, and could not be, said. And so, he says, "It is impossible for there to be propositions of ethics," and "It is clear that ethics cannot be put into words."[41] Apparently a kind of reason for this is that ethics goes beyond the limits of proper speech—it is, in that sense, transcendental.[42]

Ethical words, laws, and norms

do not express nor describe a higher range of fact, as that thinker might say who wants to save the transcendental and the distinctly different ethic by providing knowledge, or at least a proposition, about the transcendent. ... — but the world of the ethical man, of the deeply happy man, becomes for him a different world.[43]

Holmer sees this existential dimension in Wittgenstein's early work as reminiscent of Kierkegaard's emphasis on *truth as subjectivity*.

Part of the force of that grammatical remark, "truth is subjectivity," is precisely *to make one look elsewhere than in more scholarship and more doctrines* [emphasis mine] for whatever will bear out the sense of life. That "sense" and "meaning" of life that is the aim of religious teaching is an achievement of the subject, a new quality of the subject's life— new emotions, new feelings, new thoughts and chastened dispositions. The sermon obviously had to prepare a man for that newness.[44]

Therefore, the sermon, the preaching act, did not communicate directly if by direct one means communicates a body of facts, or knowledge, or information about the world in discursive prose or as propositions picturing the world to us. Rather, it serves to point to the inwardness attendant in all moral and religious understanding. So preaching is venturesome precisely because of what the words in a sermon do not do. They seemingly fail as public words.

So when words are put together, they do very well by telling us what is so about public matters. The truths of history and of the natural science seem to be public enough; but the themes of religion and of morality, those endeavors that require inwardness and individuality, put a genuine strain upon the public words.[45]

So a sermon was venturesome, like Wittgenstein's elucidations, as—"temporary helps to be discarded once used." "Indeed, they are venturesome, but mostly because they ask one to try to say what one himself cannot intellectually justify."[46]

More Venturesome Still ...

Yet this is not the end of the story. Though preaching is genuinely venturesome in so far as words do not speak in any direct way to the moral and religious domain, they nonetheless speak. And, according to Holmer, as Kierkegaard's thought continues to develop, there is an important shift that takes place in what he is prepared to say about religious communication. For Kierkegaard it begins to look as though "words were supposed to be—about something—but now they were not 'about' in any simple way. They were not communication in that direct sense at all. Instead, they were clues to the inwardness of the user of the words and had to be understood as such."[47]

In *Section III* of his essay, Holmer believes, as Kierkegaard's thought matures, he develops ideas about indirect communication that go beyond the mere recognition of the logical oddity of religious and sermonic language. Kierkegaard even gives up on the idea that speaking *about* God is inherently problematic, and shifts his focus to an appreciation of the distinction between speaking "about" in the sense that one is trying to convey information, knowledge, and a form of speaking, the point of which is the appropriation of a *capacity*.

> Kierkegaard's point, now, is that a sermon can indeed be "about" whatever you choose but that its aim is not the "truth"—otherwise it would be a lecture. Its indirection is not created by its anomalous relation to its subject matter. Even God can be talked about, Kierkegaard thinks; and, at least, the failure in talking about Him is not an inadequacy in the very structure and nature of words themselves. ... one wants the hearer to realize a capacity that may be latent within him."[48]

Because ...

> Whereas once it looked as if to know God was something like knowing in general—one might have a way of talking about knowledge of God, as if it could be conveyed directly from man to man—now it was clear that there was no knowledge of God quite like that with only the inward appropriation

to follow. Instead the realization of the capacities to fear, to love, to hope, to believe, is to make men into true subjects and new creatures. This is, then, what makes the sermon so venturesome. And knowing God is loving, fearing, hoping in a rich variety of ways.[49]

Holmer contends that as Kierkegaard's thinking develops, that speaking in the *about* mode begins to make a kind of sense. Beginning with Kierkegaard's edifying discourses, a different appreciation emerges that makes important conceptual distinctions, signaled earlier in the *Postscript*.

there will always remain a decisive difference between the poet and the religious speaker, in that the poet has no other telos than the psychological truth of his description and the art of his presentation, while the speaker has at the same time the "principal" aim of transforming everything into edification. The poet loses himself in the delineation of passion, but for the religious speaker this is but the first step; the next step is for him the decisive one, namely, to force the obstreperous individual to lay down his arms, to soften, to clear up; in short to translate everything into terms of edification.[50]

Kierkegaard did not see his own upbuilding discourses as sermons, of course, because he spoke, "as one without authority." But Holmer notes in *Section III* the importance of recognizing the venturesome character of preaching in the subjectivity of both the hearer and the speaker.

> His point is, rather, that the sermon surely must tell the truth ... But telling the truth is not all there is to it. One wants the hearer not to luxuriate in the truth, ... ; instead, one wants the hearer to realize a capacity that may be latent within him.[51]

In order for the hearer to hear, the speaker must use everything at her disposal to "awaken" the hearer to new possibilities.

> In a long essay, Kierkegaard concludes that communicating what you know is one thing, but communicating a capacity is another. A sermon must use anything and everything, truths about God and the world if you will, with an eye to making men capable of something that they presently lack.[52]

And for Kierkegaard, this capacity must extend beyond the potential hearer of the Word; it must also be reflected in the speaker as well.

> The communication is indirect, but now the notion of "indirectness" gets a different lie. Whatever one says is not quite complete in itself. But that is not all that one is after. The very life of the speaker, the context that he provides, is ever important.[53]

So as Holmer sees it, the venturesomeness of preaching rests in part on the tension that is a consequence of the speaker's words and his or her own life with them. And they are, Holmer says, "most perfect when it causes the hearer to become a new creature. Thus a capacity is stirred within him, a capacity for a new life." William H. Willimon, in his well-known textbook for pastors, has learned this lesson well.

> My colleague Richard Lischer notes that in most of our seminary preparation we preachers are taught to step back from the text, to attempt to assume a detached, cool, objective, and dispassionate disposition toward the text—scripture as a cadaver to be dissected. In the African American church, says Lischer, the pastor attempts to step into the text, try on the text, walk around in it, assuming some of the roles depicted in the text. The pastor, in preaching, leads the church in stepping into the text trying on the text, assuming a world in which the text's description of reality is more real than that which we typically privilege as "real".[54]

This "stepping into" to which Willimon and Lischer direct our attention is not a performance. Rather it is a kind of wearing, or living out, or taking up into one's life what is significant for faith, giving the form and character of the various capacities constitutive of truth belief. This feature of Holmer's analysis is given greater force in the last section of his essay.

Venturesome Revisited ...

In the last part of his essay, *Section IV*, Holmer returns to Wittgenstein's later work as a kind of recapitulation of Kierkegaard's emphasis on the logical character of religious language and by extension, on that of preaching. Contrasting Wittgenstein's earlier period with aspects of what was most significant in his later philosophy, Holmer points us to the logical significance of the relation between the preacher's language and the uses, doings, capacities, and forms of life that logically must constitute the preachers words, if they are to have theological meaning. Holmer argues, that in Wittgenstein's earlier work,

> there was a kind of objective and given relation between a simple word and a simple fact in the world. Out of these relations the complexities of true sentences could be understood. Furthermore, a logical form, in words and things, seemed to Wittgenstein to explain the picturing power of language and almost independently of the user and his wishes.

But now in Wittgenstein's later philosophy,

> he [Wittgenstein] notes what he had previously overlooked. Words have to be taken up, to be handled, to be pressed to uses, in order that you say something with them. But it also

must be clear to you, sometime in the process, that they are so being taken up, handled, and used. This is why you must have an ear for the way, the manner, the orientation and purposes of the speaker. You have to know something of the game he is playing. Otherwise the words fall dead.[55]

If we view in some detail one of the more extended treatments on Christian *believing* we have from Wittgenstein's later work, we can see explicitly how Holmer's invocation of Wittgenstein's later philosophy serves to clarify the ways in which Kierkegaard's idea that *preaching is a venturesome thing* is to be understood.

Venturing an Example

In his later work, Wittgenstein advocates for an appreciation of the context in which religious assertions are made. By so doing we see that the logical character of *religious beliefs* is different than the logical character of beliefs established as *historical facts*, for example. According to Wittgenstein:

In religious discourse we use such expressions as: "I believe that so and so will happen," and use them differently to the way in which we use them in science. Although there is a great temptation to think we do. Because we do talk of evidence, and do talk of evidence by experience. We could even talk of historic events. It has been said that Christianity rests on an historic basis. It has been said a thousand times by intelligent people that indubitability is not enough in this case. Even if there is as much evidence as for Napoleon. Because the indubitability wouldn't be enough to make me change my whole life. It doesn't rest on an historic basis in the sense that the ordinary belief in historic facts could serve as a foundation. Here we have a belief in historic facts different from a belief in ordinary historic facts.[56]

Remembering the close logical relation Holmer makes between theology and preaching, Holmer makes the following claim:

Theology does not at every juncture demand an historical understanding before it can be reasserted in our day. To make that case supposed far too standardized a view ... there may be instances of literature, New Testament and Old, Shakespeare, Moliere, or Plato, where one needs to know the time and occasion before one gets the drift of what was said. But these are particular instances where historical understanding is a necessary priority. Most instances of the New Testament, for example, are not like that. One suspects that it is far more important than most historical material to learn to hunger and thirst for righteousness, to learn to love a neighbor, and to achieve a high degree of self-concern, in order to understand the religious themes of the New Testament.[57]

What Wittgenstein and Holmer are arguing is that it is a deep conceptual confusion to conflate the logical character of historical truths with that of religious truths; that the logical character of historical beliefs cannot establish the *kind of truth* that is indicative of religious belief. Historical truths are by definition *contingent*. Religious truths, by contrast, are not. That is, religious beliefs do not *have* the logical character of contingent truths. But it is not a matter of historical criteria being inadequate to the task of evaluating religious claims. Rather, it is a matter of the historical *proof game* being out of place. Wittgenstein puts the matter this way:

> Christianity is not based on a historical truth; rather, it offers us a (historical) narrative and says: now believe! But not, believe this narrative with the belief appropriate to a historical narrative, rather, through thick and thin, which you can do only as the result of a life. *Here you have a narrative, don't take the same attitude to it as you take to other historical narratives!* Make a *quite different* place in your life for it.— There is nothing *paradoxical* about that![58]

As Wittgenstein argues, the conditions for accepting the "truth" of Christian assertions are connected with the way in which they inform the life of the believer. Or, to put the matter another way, the grammar of religious truths is not the same as the grammar of historical truths. But because the words "truth," "reality," and "fact" are sometimes used in religious assertions, it is too often assumed by apologists and critics alike that what we have is a uniform criterion of rationality. Wittgenstein asks that before we assume that the logic of the two uses of "truth" or "fact" or "reality" are the same that we look to see how these words are used in their respective contexts. As Wittgenstein has it, "Those people who had faith didn't apply the doubt which would ordinarily apply to *any* historical propositions. Especially propositions of a time long past, etc."[59]

Karl Barth, it seems, would agree:

The Resurrection is therefore an occurrence in history, which took place outside the gates of Jerusalem in the year A. D. 30, in as much as there "came to pass," was discovered and recognized. But inasmuch as the occurrence was conditioned by the Resurrection, in so far, that is, as it was not he "coming to pass," or the discovery, or the recognition, which conditioned its necessity and appearance and revelation, *the Resurrection is not an event in history at all* (emphasis mine). Jesus is *declared to be the Son of God* wherever He reveals Himself and is recognized as the Messiah.[60]

Barth is among the most important theological voices of the twentieth century. Although Wittgenstein's work does not appear to be known to Barth, both Wittgenstein and Barth share the same perspective on the incommensurate logical character of religious and historical truths.[61] Barth wants to draw our attention to the fact that saying that the resurrection of Jesus has *come to pass* is not necessarily to invoke historical criteria in the analysis of its truth. Barth is not denying that the "resurrection" *happened in the past*. What he is emphasizing is that whatever the meaning of the resurrection's having "come to pass," it cannot be properly understood in terms of historical criteria. Barth's comments point to the internal relationship between the truth of Jesus's resurrection and coming to see him as *the Son of God*. To say that Jesus is the Son of God is to make a very different place in one's life for this truth.

Barth, like Wittgenstein, wants to reject the imposition of alien criteria in the investigation of theological language. Barth's concern is with the intrusion of criteria which are thought to transcend criteria given with the Church's talk about God. To introduce alien criteria of meaning into the investigation of the Church's language about God is inevitably to distort the meaning of that language.

> [T]he historian, the educationist, and so on, and not least the philosopher himself, for all their goodwill in taking this matter into account, always, within the framework of their own sciences, speak past the problem here confronting them. In other words, they judge the Church's language about God

on principles foreign to it, instead of on its own principles, and thus *increase instead of diminishing the harm on account of which the Church needs a critical science.*[62]

What Barth objects to is the way in which philosophers, historians, and scientists, etc. appropriate criteria internal to the interest of their respective disciplines in the investigation of the meaning of the Church's talk about God. For Barth, the consequences of this kind of theological investigation are not the clarification of the Church's talk about God, but its distortion. In the Quest for the historical Jesus movement in Biblical studies, for example, the exaltation of the canons of historical research led to the inevitable divorce between the historical Jesus and the Christ of faith. To Barth's mind, this result is intolerable. "Within history, Jesus as the Christ can be understood only as Problem or Myth."[63] By contrast Barth asserts:

This declaration by the Son of Man to be the Son of God is the significance of Jesus, and apart from this, Jesus has no more significance or insignificance than may be attached to any man or thing or period of history in itself.[64]

Barth is not rejecting history per se. He is rejecting the notion that what "believing in the truth" of Jesus as the Son of God comes to, what it means to speak of the divine, or with the voice of faith or with religious conviction is not given with the limits of historical research, or any other science. It is, as Barth suggests, to look "past the problem here confronting them." But if not rational or historical in character, then what is the logical character of the language to which Barth so emphatically alludes? Wittgenstein is helpful here. Even if the evidence of Jesus's resurrection were as indubitable as Napoleon's reign, what "believing" in that context would come to would not be what "believing" means for the religious believer. Believing in the resurrection is to believe, not because of the strength of the "evidence," but *with a life*. Indeed, Wittgenstein asks:

> What inclines even me to believe in Christ's Resurrection? It is as though I play with the thought—If he did not rise from the dead, then he decomposed in the grave like any other man. He is *dead and decomposed*. In that case he is a teacher like any other and can no longer *help*; and once more we are orphaned and alone. So we have to content ourselves with wisdom and speculation. We are in a sort of hell where we can do nothing but dream, roofed in, as it were, and cut off from heaven. But if I am to be REALLY saved—what I need is *certainty* not wisdom, dreams or speculation—and this certainty is faith. And faith is faith in what is needed by my *heart*, my *soul*, not my speculative intelligence.[65]

Here we see that for Wittgenstein the imposition of alien criteria, i.e., the canons of historical inquiry, is out of place with respect to the question of the truth of the resurrection of Jesus. And he is joined in this by Karl Barth who himself locates its truth outside the canons of historical inquiry. Rather the proper context for religious or theological meaning and therefore the assessment of theological truths is properly located in the subjectivity of the believer and the wider religious context within which the believer operates.

> For it is my soul with its passions, as it were with its flesh and blood, that has to be saved, not my abstract mind. Perhaps we can say: Only *love* can believe the Resurrection. Or: It is *love* that believes the Resurrection. We might say: Redeeming love believes even in the Resurrection; holds fast even to the Resurrection. What combats doubt is, as it were, *redemption*. Holding fast to *this* must be holding fast to that belief. So what that means is: first you must be redeemed and hold on to your redemption (keep hold of your redemption)—then you will see that you are holding fast to this belief.[66]

Wittgenstein is inviting us to see that the sense of religious belief in the resurrection of Jesus is given with the way in which it informs the whole of a person's life. It has the "truth" of informing the whole of a person's life, of governing the way one sees the world and oneself. John Whittaker has summarized this logical characteristic of religious belief well:

one can believe in them [religious truths] only by following them, by abiding in them, by converting to them, like one adheres to a set of principles that founds an entirely new way of looking at things. Since such ideas regulate a whole new framework of judgement, coming to believe in them is not an outgrowth of a way of thinking that one already understands, as would be the case if the beliefs at issue were hypotheses to be judged on familiar historical or scientific ground. No; in this case believing requires reconfiguring one's thinking, as the regulative beliefs at issue represent the gateway to a whole new manner of seeing.[67]

This notion of "a whole new manner of seeing" is brought out nicely by Peter Winch in his treatment of Lessing and the stories of Jesus resurrection. Winch points us to the curious story of Jesus's disciples on the road to Emmaus. If anyone should have recognized Jesus it would be those who had followed him. Of course, it is plausible, given Jesus's death only a few days before, that the experience of his horrific death "made them incapable of countenancing the possibility that he might be this fellow traveler."[68] But this feature of the story is negated by the disciples having, earlier that day, heard from the women who were at the tomb, reporting that Jesus was alive. "One might rather think that this would have made them more receptive to recognizing Jesus when he appeared to them on the road."[69] Winch wants to insist that the point of raising these questions is not to cast doubt on the veracity of the resurrection story. To the contrary, the point of the questions is to assess *what kind of story it is?* To do that, one must, Winch suggests, ask: "what then is the point of the story?"

> I could only point to what in fact is done with it in the religious context to which it belongs: to the Christian practice of commemorating the meeting on the road to Emmaus by asking a stranger into one's home to share a meal, to the kinds of sermon preached on this particular text, to the ways in which the scene has been variously represented in religious art, and so on.[70]

To press the point just a bit further, one could say that to receive or believe in the truth of the Resurrection is, for one thing, to welcome the stranger. The welcome of the stranger is a major theological theme in the Bible and the Christian tradition.[71] One might argue that to "get in on" the Christian faith, in part, is to see how the welcome of the stranger informs the whole of one's life. And the stories around the Resurrection of Jesus serve to picture the significance of this particular religious capacity.

And Whittaker's notion of "a whole new manner of seeing" is reminiscent, again, of the language Barth sometimes invoked to stress the distinctive logical character of religious believing; Barth's "strange new world within the Bible."[72]

Echoing Barth, Willimon says, "Part of the joy of being a biblical preacher is that we get a front-row seat on the spectacle of the creation of a new world. The Bible wants to give us new experiences, to create a new reality that would have been unavailable to us without the Bible."[73] "So, too, [Holmer argues] it is with sermons." "The words do not tell you everything, not because they fail, but because the 'everything' is not one more subject matter. Sometimes, it is a matter of becoming quiet, just, hopeful, loving, and faithful to God Almighty."[74]

A Venturesome Conclusion

Following Kierkegaard and Wittgenstein, it now appears, there *is* a sense in which preaching in the *about* mode is warranted, if by *about* one means the engendering of certain capacities, heretofore unknown, unavailable, or absent to one's subjectivity. The preacher must preach in such a way as to elicit new possibilities for her hearer. And the preacher must recognize that her own subjectivity is part of the mix; that the words of the preacher must connect up with the kind of life that is both enacted in the pulpit and lived out in one's own life. "It would be most terrible, most venturesome, to speak too easily without ever considering that what one is talking about becomes nonsensical if that subject, namely oneself, does not bear it out." And even where the force of one's preaching is not at all times and in every way borne out by one's own life, then there is always the importance of Scripture itself and the lives of the Apostles, Holmer tells us. And to say this, Holmer insists, is to acknowledge a certain reality beyond one's self, a "someone" as he has it, to whom "we must turn." "Then," he says, "one preaches without the expectation of very much glory for oneself and less precisely to the degree that one does it well."[75] And in this respect, above all else, *preaching is a venturesome thing*. "The words fade away and one is left with not the adequacy of the words in question but the adequacy of one's life before God."[76]

Notes

1. I was Phillips' student and attaché for the term, driving him here and there (he did not drive), and helping negotiate some of the more practical aspects of living in New Haven.

2. D.Z. Phillips, *Faith after Foundationalism* (New York: Routledge, 1988).

3. D.Z. Phillips, "Lindbeck's Audience," *Modern Theology*, October, 1987. This is the paper Phillips gave in the Common Room discussion. The paper was later revised and expanded in his *Faith after Foundationalism*.

4. George Lindbeck, *The Nature of Doctrine* (Philadelphia: The Westminster Press, 1984).

5 D.Z. Phillips, "Holmer's Audience," later appeared as "Grammarians and Guardians" in a *festschrift* for Paul Holmer, *The Grammar of the Heart*, ed. Richard H. Bell (New York: Harper & Row, 1988). The material in that article is revised and expanded in Phillips's *Faith after Foundationalism*.

6 Paul L. Holmer, *The Grammar of Faith* (New York: Harper & Row, 1978).

7 Phillips, *Faith after Foundationalism*, p.x.

8 Mark Horst, "Paul Holmer: A Profile," *Christian Century*, 105.29, October 12, 1988, pp. 891–5.

9 Paul L. Homer, *The Paul L. Holmer Papers: On Kierkegaard and the Truth, Vol. I*, ed. David J Gouwens and Lee C. Barrett III (Eugene, OR: Cascade Books, Wipf and Stock Publishers, 2012), p. xv.

10 Stanley Hauerwas, "How to Go on When You Know You Are Going to Be Misunderstood, or How Paul Holmer Ruined My Life, or Making Sense of Paul Holmer," in *Wilderness Wanderings: Probing Twentieth-Century Theology and Philosophy*, Radical Traditions: Theology in a Postcritical Key (Boulder, CO: Westview, 1997), pp. 143–52.

11 Richard H. Bell, ed. *The Grammar of the Heart: New Essays in Moral Philosophy and Theology* (San Francisco: Harper & Row, 1988). Based on the March 1987 symposium: "The Grammar of the Heart: Thinking with Kierkegaard and Wittgenstein," to honor Paul L. Holmer, held at The College of Wooster, Wooster, Ohio, p. xiii.

12 Holmer, *The Grammar of Faith*, p. xi.

13 Ibid., pp. 68, 69.

14 D.Z. Phillips, in Bell, p. 24.

15 D.Z. Phillips, "Grammarians and Guardians," in *The Grammar of the Heart: New Essays in Moral Philosophy and Theology,* ed., Richard H. Bell (San Francisco: Harper & Row, 1988), pp. 21–35.

16 D.Z. Phillips, in Bell, p. 21.

17 Holmer, *The Grammar of Faith*, p. 152.

18 Phillips, *Faith after Foundationalism*, p. 228. (The reader will find here an expanded discussion of the same issues over two chapters, "Grammar without Foundations," pp. 225-37, and "Grammarians and Guardians," pp. 238-54.

19 Ibid., p. 229.

20 Holmer, *The Grammar of Faith*, p. 9.

21 Phillips, *Faith after Foundationalism*, pp. 229-31.

22 Phillips, *Faith after Foundationalism*, p. 231.

23 Paul L. Holmer, *The Grammar of Faith*, p. 145.

24 Paul L. Holmer, *The Paul L. Holmer Papers, Vol.III, Communicating the Faith Indirectly: Selected, Sermons, Addresses, and Prayers*, ed. David J. Gouwens and Lee C. Barrett III (Eugene, OR: Cascade Books, 2012).

25 Paul L. Holmer, "Indirect Communication: Something about the Sermon (With References to Kierkegaard and Wittgenstein)," in *The Paul L. Holmer Papers, Vol.III, Communicating the Faith Indirectly: Selected, Sermons, Addresses, and Prayers*, ed. David J. Gouwens and Lee C. Barrett III (Eugene, OR: Cascade Books, 2012).

26 David Gouwens and Lee C. Barrett III, "Editor's Preface," in Paul L. Holmer, *The Paul L. Holmer Papers, Vol.III, Communicating the Faith Indirectly: Selected, Sermons, Addresses, and Prayers*, ed. David J. Gouwens and Lee C. Barrett III (Eugene, OR: Cascade Books, 2012), p. xiv.

27 Mark Horst, *The Christian Century*, October 12, 1988, pp. 891-5.

28 William H. Willimon, "Forward" to Paul L. Holmer, *Communicating the Faith Indirectly*, p. xv.

29 Paul L. Holmer, "Indirect Communication: Something about the Sermon (With References to Kierkegaard and Wittgenstein)," p. 3.

30 Ibid., p. 4.

31 Ibid., p. 4.

32 Ibid., p. 5.

33 Ibid., p. 5.

34 Ibid., p. 5.

35 Ibid., pp. 5–6.

36 Ibid., p. 4.

37 Ibid., pp. 6–7.

38 Ludwig Wittgenstein, *Tractatus Logico-Philosophicus*, trans. D. F. Pears and B. F. McGuinness (London: Routledge & Kegan Paul, 1922), paras.6.522 and 6.53.

39 Holmer, "Indirect Communication," p. 7.

40 Ibid., p. 8.

41 Ludwig Wittgenstein, *Tractatus Logico-Philosophicus*, trans. D. F. Pears and B. F. McGuinness (London: Routledge & Kegan Paul, 1922), paras. 6.42 and 6.421.

42 Ibid., pp. 8, 9.

43 Ibid., p. 9.

44 Ibid., p. 10.

45 Ibid., p. 12.

46 Ibid., p. 13.

47 Ibid., p. 12.

48 Ibid., p. 14.

49 Ibid., p. 15.

50 Soren Kierkegaard, *Concluding Unscientific Postscript*, trans. David Swenson and Walter Lowrie (Princeton: Princeton University Press, 1941), p. 230.

51 Holmer, "Indirect Communication," p. 14.

52 Ibid., p. 13.

53 Ibid., p. 14.

54 William H. Willimon, *Pastor: The Theology and Practice of Ordained Ministry*, Revised Edition (Nashville, TN: Abingdon Press, 2016), p. 125. I do not think Holmer would embrace Lindbeck's notion of "re-description of reality" but the idea of a "new reality" is germane.

55 Paul L. Homer, "Indirect Communication: Something about the Sermon," pp. 17–18.

56 Ludwig Wittgenstein, *Wittgenstein: Lectures and Conversations on Aesthetics, Psychology & Religious Belief*, ed. Cyril Barrett (Oxford: Basil Blackwell, 1966), p. 57.

57 Homer, *The Grammar of Faith*, p. 9.

58 Ludwig Wittgenstein, *Culture and Value*, ed. G. H. von Wright, trans. Peter Winch (Chicago: The University of Chicago Press, 1980), p. 32e.

59 Wittgenstein, *Wittgenstein: Lectures*, p. 57.

60 Karl Barth, *The Epistle to the Romans* (Oxford: Oxford University Press, 1968), pp. 30.

61 See D.Z. Phillips, *Faith after Foundationalism*, pp. 226–7 and Jeffrey G. Willetts, *Karl Barth and Philosophy: The Grammatical Aim and Character of His Theology.*, PhD dissertation, University of Wales, Swansea, 1996.

62 Karl Barth, *Church Dogmatics*, I/1 (Edinburgh: T&T Clark, 1936), p. 5 [emphasis mine].

63 Barth, *The Epistle to the Romans*, p. 30.

64 Ibid.

65 Ludwig Wittgenstein, *Culture and Value*, ed. G. H. von Wright, trans. Peter Winch (Chicago: The University of Chicago Press, 1980), p. 33e.

66 Ibid.

67 John H. Whittaker, "'At the End of Reason Come Persuasion,'" in *The Possibilities of Sense: Essays in Honour of D.Z. Phillips*, ed. John Whittaker (Basingstoke, Hampshire, and New York: Palgrave MacMillan, 2002), p. 143.

68 Peter Winch, "Lessing and the Resurrection," in *The Possibilities of Sense: Essays in Honour of D.Z. Phillips*, ed. John H. Whittaker (Basingstoke, Hampshire, and New York: Palgrave, 2002), p. 192.

69 Ibid., p. 192.

70 Ibid.

71 In the past decade interest in the theme of Hospitality and in particular the idea of "welcoming the stranger" has become a major topic of intellectual and spiritual interest, which a cursory review of recent theological publications will reveal.

72 Karl Barth, "The Strange New World within the Bible," in *The Word of God and the Word of Man,* trans. Douglas Horton (Glouster, MA: Peter Smith, 1978), pp. 28–50.

73 Willimon, *Pastor: The Theology and Practice of Ordained Ministry*, p. 124.

74 Holmer, *Communicating the Faith Indirectly*, pp. 18–19.

75 Ibid., p. 19.

76 Ibid.

5
Paul Holmer and Theology as Grammar

Ryan Duerr

Introduction

In §373 of the *Philosophical Investigations*, Ludwig Wittgenstein followed up his remark about how "Grammar tells what kind of object anything is" with an intriguing parenthetical: "(Theology as grammar.)"[1] To the chagrin of many philosophers and theologians alike who would come after him, Wittgenstein offered no further explicit clarification of how theology might be understood as "grammar." Those who have carefully worked their way through the aporetic pedagogy of the *Investigations* will have a good sense of Wittgenstein's use of the word, "grammar." And those who are familiar with the details of this Austrian philosopher's life will not be surprised that a comment about theology worked its way into his philosophical work.[2] Nevertheless, these three words—"theology as grammar," or "*Theologie als Gramatik*" in the original German—have sparked more than a little confusion, speculation, and controversy in the years since Wittgenstein's *Philosophical Investigations* were posthumously published in 1953.

Like most trail-blazing thinkers throughout history, Wittgenstein's thought has been variously unpacked, interpreted, and extended—and this has been done in divergent ways toward incommensurate ends. Unsurprisingly, the appropriation and application of Wittgenstein's thought by theologians has, likewise, been polyvalent. This might leave students of philosophical theology wondering how exactly Wittgenstein's therapeutic philosophical method ought to be brought to bear on the theological task and what sort of fruit it might produce. Indeed, the intellectual trajectory of certain heirs to Wittgenstein's philosophical mantle might even dissuade such students from a Wittgensteinian approach to theological method altogether.

Nevertheless, hope for such a method and for an elucidation of what Wittgenstein meant when he suggested that theology might be understood as "grammar" is not lost. There are a number of theologians who have internalized Wittgenstein's method and faithfully brought it to bear on contemporary theology. In particular, this paper shall argue that one such reliable projection of Wittgenstein's thought into theology can be found in the work of Paul Holmer, especially his collection of essays entitled *The Grammar of Faith*.

Paul L. Holmer (1916–2004) taught philosophy for over forty years, first as professor of philosophy at the University of Minnesota from 1946 to 1960 and then as professor of philosophical theology at Yale Divinity School from 1960 to 1987. He wrote extensively on the topics of truth, faith, and the intersection of theology with the scientific study of religion and was most well known for his work on the Danish philosopher, Søren Kierkegaard. However, Holmer was also one of the earliest American intellectuals to recognize the potential help that Wittgenstein's philosophy might offer Christian theologians who increasingly found themselves getting caught up in the muddled thinking of modern philosophy.[3] Holmer penned a number of essays examining the nature, substance, and problems of theology from an explicitly Wittgensteinian perspective. Many of these were brought together in a book, the title of which (i.e., *The Grammar of Faith*) eponymously gestured toward Wittgenstein's comment about "theology as grammar."[4] The aim of Holmer's essays, one might say, was to draw upon Wittgenstein's thought in order "to shew the [theological] fly out of the [philosophical] fly-bottle."[5]

In the pages which follow, I will argue that Holmer's writings on Wittgenstein offer contemporary theologians a faithful projection of Ludwig Wittgenstein's philosophical method to problems which have beset modern theology in the modern era. First, I will argue that Holmer successfully extends Wittgenstein's criticism of modern philosophy's quest for philosophical "foundations" to modern theology's attempt to lay a conceptual foundation of "facts" or "the concept of being"—an intellectual endeavor which Holmer refers to collectively as "theism." Second, I will show how this leads Holmer to follow Wittgenstein's oblique suggestion that theology functions as grammar rightly by pointing him away from the realm of conceptual abstraction to the ordinary language of Christian faith and leading him to (re-)root theology in the concreteness of Christian living. Then, I will attend to the ways in which Holmer's Wittgensteinian trajectory leads him to see the aim of Christian theology as the transformation of one's life, a theme which echoes Wittgenstein's insistence that the conceptual transformation required by his therapeutic method of philosophy was ultimately a form of "work on oneself."[6] And finally, I will explore the way that Holmer tapped into Wittgenstein's final writings on epistemology in order to offer a view of certainty as grounded in pre-theoretical practices and ways of life (as opposed to basic theistic propositions) as well as to commend a retrieval of thick Christian practice as a Wittgensteinian way of addressing modern religious doubt.

Theology and Philosophical Foundations

Central to Ludwig Wittgenstein's philosophical project was his rejection of philosophy as some sort of super-science. In §§115–116 of the *Philosophical Investigations*, Wittgenstein critiques this picture of philosophy and adumbrates the trajectory of his later "therapeutic" philosophical method:

> 115. A *picture* held us captive. And we could not get outside it, for it lay in our language and language seemed to repeat it to us inexorably.
>
> 116. When philosophers use a word—"knowledge," "being," "object," "I," "proposition," "name"—and try to grasp the *essence* of the thing, one must always ask oneself: is the word ever actually used in this way in the language which is its original home?
>
> What *we* do is to bring words back from their metaphysical to their everyday use.[7]

For Wittgenstein, modern philosophy's attempt to flee into abstraction for the sake of securing knowledge on an edifice of universality had blinded philosophers to the irreducible situatedness of meaning within particular language-games. It led them to conceive of philosophy as a discipline that was somehow able to uncover a basic and universal language which undergirded the variety of parochial language-games found in everyday life.

Wittgenstein received his philosophical training under Bertrand Russell at Cambridge. At the time, Russell was a leading light in the burgeoning discipline of analytic philosophy, and his *Principia Mathematica* had sought to derive mathematics from self-evident principles of logic. Wittgenstein had become fascinated with certain problems that Russell had encountered in his work and went to study with Russell at Cambridge.[8] For a time, Russell believed that Wittgenstein would succeed him as the torchbearer of analytic philosophy. However, Wittgenstein's life ended up taking him in a very different direction. Instead of carrying Russell's work forward, Wittgenstein wound up deconstructing the analytic enterprise from within. Whereas Russell sought to construct an ideal language that could serve as the foundation for all other languages, Wittgenstein began a revolution in philosophy that sought to refocus the eyes of philosophers on ordinary language.

Throughout his magnum opus, the *Philosophical Investigations*, Wittgenstein sought to help philosophers appreciate the connection between the meaning of any given word and the role that such words play in particular social contexts. By offering a series of illustrations and examples, he shows the reader how attempts at getting past ordinary language in order to secure meaning is tantamount to "saw[ing] off the branch on which [one is] sitting."[9] Meaning is ("for a *large* class of cases")[10] dependent upon use, and use is regulated by the rules of actual communities. And since understanding the use of words in language games is so determinate for their meaning, there is no meaning to be found outside of ordinary language. There is, therefore, nothing useful to be gained by seeking the sort of ideal language quested after by analytic philosophy. Any ideal language that is an actual language would turn out to be just another particular language which itself is grounded in forms of life, not other languages.[11] "What we have rather to do," says Wittgenstein, "is to *accept* the everyday language-games ... [they] need no justification; attempts at justification need to be rejected."[12]

Wittgenstein's resistance to attempts at laying down justifications for ordinary language was picked up by Paul Holmer. He saw clearly how modern theologians are tempted to justify ordinary religious language by appealing to some sort of meta-language. As Holmer explains, the rise of the scientific method along with modern, secular politics has led to the problem of the "demythologizing" of Christians Scripture and a concomitant crisis of meaning.[13] The project of demythologization seemed to undermine the *prime facie* meaningfulness of religious language.

As a result, Christian theologians began looking for some sort of new foundation beyond the (pre-scientific) language of the Bible that might re-imbue Christian language with "viable religious meanings" for the modern world.[14]

Some theologians turned to onto-theology. Their goal was to pin down some sort of *fundamentum in re* (such as Paul Tillich's ground-of-being) which could unite all things under a common term and then, in turn, be referred to God.[15] But there are two big problems with such an onto-theological turn. First, as Martin Heidegger has made clear, talk of "Being" is anything but neutral. It emerges from the particular tradition of Greek philosophy, it has a history, and it by no means has a corner on the global philosophical market. But second, and even more important for Holmer, while one might find a way to move from a notion of Being-as-such to the idea of God, it is not clear how onto-theology might re-imbue the rest of Christianity with "viable religious meaning." How can one derive the trinity, the incarnation, the sacraments, etc. from an abstract concept of Being? It would seem that Being is a vanishingly small foundation that can prop up little, if any, substantial Christian teaching.[16]

Other theologians have turned to the idea of the "brute fact" as a possible "foundation" for Christian theology. As Holmer explains, "Concepts like 'historical,' 'truth,' and 'fact' seem minimal, rock-bottom, and almost primitive and underived. Everybody claims to know that they mean—they seem to be the very furniture of our everyday talk."[17] If only Christians could pinpoint the basic "facts" of Christianity, then they would be able to build a structure of "viable religious meanings" from the ground up, so to speak, in a way that is solid, secure, and universally relevant. However, as Holmer goes on to explain, the idea of a "brute" or "atomic fact" rests on an "ill-begotten general concept" of "facts." The word "fact," does not represent a master concept of reality, but is a relative term that "always marks a distinction between what is *not* disputed 'now,' 'here,' 'in this context,' 'under these circumstances,' 'presently,' and what *is* so disputed." As such, the idea of a "fact" does not provide theologians with firm ground. It denotes a "moving line of demarcation."[18] In other words, there is no such thing as a "fact *qua* fact" because "fact" is a game-relative concept. Historical facts are historical, scientific facts are scientific, and "theological statements, finally, if reducible at all, are reducible only to theological facts."[19] What theologians mean when they say that theology is founded on "facts" is that they are trying to reduce certain basic theological ideas to historical or scientific ideas. But, as Holmer points out, this is to undermine theology as a unique language game from the very start.

Whether a theologians looks to Being or basic facts, Holmer argues that they are indulging in a delusion called "theism." Theism, for Holmer, refers to the practice of trying to ground theology with the conceptual tools of philosophy.[20] Whether those tools are more rationalistic or empirical matters little. Either which way, the goal is the same: to found Christian theology on some more basic and universal conceptual language. But, in the end, this strategy simply tends to dissolve theology into science or history. And the first casualty of any such dissolution is the ordinary language of Christianity along with the forms of life, worship, and faith that it engenders.

Over against the temptation of theism, Holmer turns to Wittgenstein and echoes his assertion about the groundlessness of language-games. Christianity "needs no justification" and "attempts at justification need to be rejected." If Christianity is in the midst of a crisis of meaning—and Holmer believes that it truly is in the midst of such a crisis—the problem is not the demythologization of scripture but the disintegration of the Christian language-game. And the solution to the problem of meaning will not be found in theism, but in a recovery of those ungrounded forms of *acting* that are the real foundation of the Christian language-game.[21]

Theology and Ordinary Language

For Wittgenstein, giving up the quest for epistemic foundations did not mean giving up philosophy but reorienting philosophy. In the *Philosophical Investigations* he offers a new understanding of philosophy as a descriptive (as opposed to normative) discipline. That is, philosophy does not found ordinary language, but seeks to clearly describe the "grammar" of ordinary language and to point out when ordinary language begins to "idle."[22] Instead of analyzing phenomena, philosophy analyzes concepts, and by analyzing concepts, philosophers set themselves about analyzing the patterned use of words in particular language-games.[23]

Wittgensteinian philosophy does not look *past* ordinary language but looks carefully *at* ordinary language and studies its "grammar." Grammar, here, means right usage according to the "rules" of particular language-games. But when it comes to spoken language (that space where philosophy does so much of its work), it is important to remember that grammar means more than right use of words vis-à-vis verbal systems. Grammar refers to right usage in the context of wholistic forms of life. Hence an analysis of ordinary language requires careful observation of the way words mesh with other words *as well as* how words mesh with practices. Only in this wholistic sense can Wittgenstein's statements about grammar in the *Philosophical Investigations* be rightly understood.[24] To attend to grammar is to attend to the patterned ways that particular communities of practice actively navigate their way through the "hurly-burly" of life.

Early on in the *Investigations*, Wittgenstein elaborates on his use of the term "language-game." Far from intending to trivialize ordinary language, Wittgenstein uses this term to "bring into prominence the fact that the *speaking* of language is part of an activity, or of a life-form."[25] When these life-forms (instead of the abstractions of modern philosophy) take center stage, the polyvalence of words becomes clear. In §11 Wittgenstein evocatively compares words to tools:

> Think of the tools in a tool box: there is a hammer, pliers, a saw, a screw-driver, a rule, a glue-pot, glue, nails and screws.— The functions of words are as diverse as the functions of these objects. (And in both cases there are similarities.) Of course, what confuses us is the uniform appearance of words when we hear them spoken or meet them in script and print. For their *application* is not presented to us so clearly. Especially when we are doing philosophy![26]

Just as games have rules and moves in games are meaningless without a grasp of those rules, so also words derive their meaning from their applications within the complexities of lived existence—the very complexities that theism tends to overlook or ignore. In order to attend to meaning, therefore, one cannot retreat into ideal language but must go ever further into the complexity and messiness of ordinary language in ordinary life.

For Holmer, it is precisely a closer attention to the ordinary language of Christianity that is needed to overcome the crisis of meaning that the church faces in modernity. Theism leads Christians into the land of abstraction and ideal language, and the result is an anemic Christianity. It proceeds according to a "very plausible dogma" in modern philosophy, namely, "that meanings are kinds of events, objects, persons, or things lying behind language and for which language is supposed to stand ... All of language, verbal and written, is [therefore] a symbolic activity."[27] But this notion of language makes language out to be nothing but a medium of representation of things that are nonlinguistic. In other words, this view of meaning takes the *use* of words in scientific and historical language-games and acts as if these are the *only genuine* uses of words (i.e., their only real meanings). In contrast, Holmer proffers a Wittgensteinian observation: "There is no single philosophy of language, no single explanation of how meanings are bestowed, for there is no conceptual scheme, behind words, that can be grasped by the special tools of abstract reflection, dialectic, or subtle inference" (all of which, of course, are done in language). Rather, "meanings are an intimate part of the situation in which language is used, where speakers and writers talk in order to secure the listeners' and readers' responses. Meanings have no other status and location than that."[28] By failing to attend to the context of religious language in a thick way, Christian theologians (under the influence of theists) have allowed the meanings (i.e., correct usages) of Christian language to get lost in the rush for "epistemic foundations." And in doing so, they cause what they hope to prevent.

Holmer points out that most religious words gain their meaning "only when their role is pronounced. If there is no role, they too drop away."[29] When students are taught technical scientific terminology out of a text book, for example, they are bound to forget it unless those words "come to life" in the lab. Only when the situations for which the vocabulary was formulated are experienced will the terms come to mean for the students what they mean to scientists in the field. And the same is true of religion. Without active participation in worship, prayer, confession, forgiveness, sharing the Gospel, ethical living, etc. religious words are unable to retain their theological meaning. Unfortunately, since "metaphysics has pretended to lay hold of a kind of conceptual cogitation in its purest and least sullied form, it has been held that metaphysics … [as opposed to Christian practice] discloses the meaning of Scripture, hymns, and the rest of religious language."[30]

In order to recover Christian meanings, therefore, Holmer advises theologians to take a Wittgensteinian turn. Theology must cease to be a quest to escape from ordinary Christian life and language and must instead attend to the "grammar of faith." We must admit that "there is no short road to restoring meanings."[31] Instead, Christian living must be rehabilitated and theologians must be its grammarians.

Theology and Godliness

Wittgenstein once wrote in one of his notebooks that "work on philosophy—like work in architecture in many respects—is really more work on oneself. On one's own conception. On how one sees things. (And what one expects of them.)"[32] Conceptual clarity requires self-involvement because meaning is bound up in use. As such, a person does not actually know what a word means unless they know how it is used. And in this context, "know" refers to tacit "know-how" as opposed to explicit "know-that." To claim that a person knows how to hit a baseball because they are familiar with the principles of physics that govern the arch of a small, dense sphere and the rotations of long wooden sticks is absurd. Sure, this person knows something scientific about physical interactions, but that is not what is meant when someone asks if a person knows how to hit a baseball. To know how to hit a baseball requires experience, practice, and skill. This sort of knowledge is tacit and can only be acquired through training—that is, by "working on oneself."

For Wittgenstein, understanding requires intentional involvement. Abstract principles, therefore, can be useful, but their usefulness is primarily heuristic. They are not ready-made bits of trans-contextual knowledge but require skilled application in particular circumstances under certain conditions. Rather, they often require "expert judgement" in their application due to the inevitable "indefiniteness" that faces people in real-world situations.[33] In other words, even "know-that" is only as good as a person's already-acquired "know-how."[34]

Here, Holmer once again manages to project Wittgenstein's thought faithfully into theology. According to Holmer, since "all which adds to the working and viability of speech, be it behavior, gesture, circumstances, responses, references, or all kinds of accompaniments, also makes language meaningful," the crisis of religious meaning is the result of a loss of *social* and *embodied* religious practice. "The task for theologians, then, if they decry the vacuousness of religious language in the pulpit and the pew, is not to sketch a theory that will impart meaning as much as it is to suggest the 'learning how' and all that that involved in the religious life."[35] The crisis of meaning that the church faces in the modern world is caused not by its lack of rational foundations but by its abstraction of religious language from religious life (and, perhaps, the imposition of modern scientific and historical forms of life upon religious language).

The theological meaning of knowing God cannot be replaced by a scientific meaning—indeed, since "No one has ever seen God," there can be no scientific meaning for the word, "God."[36] A grammatical understanding of "God" within Christianity requires know-how that is developed in prayer, worship, receiving the sacraments, and living out the Christian life. One learns what the word "God" means when one is persecuted for the sake of Christ, when one turns the other cheek, when one confesses their sins before their Christian brothers and sisters, etc. Without these practices, Christianity loses its meaning and either fizzles away into irrelevance (like how students forget all of the scientific terminology that they learned in high school unless they *use* it in the years that follow) or gets highjacked by the grammar of a different language-game (such as theism, nationalism, etc.).

Restoring meaning to Christian language, therefore, requires ethical transformation, according to Holmer. It requires a revivification of Christian practice as the only setting within which Christian words are imbued with their theological meaning and become proper Christian concepts. Theology is the "grammar of faith" and entails "working on oneself." It requires attention to and participation in Christian forms of life, and it order to do so, it must turn away from the escapist metaphysics of theism and toward participation in Christian practice.

A New Kind of Certainty

Does setting aside the theistic quest for a meta-language that can provide epistemic foundations mean that Christians are prone to flounder in interminable uncertainty, fideistically clinging to a religious form of life that they have no good reason to hold on to? Holmer, following Wittgenstein, recognizes that this sort of either/or no longer finds purchase once the modern philosophical obsession with foundationalist metaphysics is dissolved.

Near the end of his life, Wittgenstein turn explicitly to questions of epistemology in a series of four notebooks that were posthumously collected and published under the title, *On Certainty*. Just as Wittgenstein, earlier on, challenged analytic philosophy's tendency to treat matters of thought and meaning as "taking place in a queer kind of medium, the mind"[37] that was disconnected from the communal life of actual languages, in *On Certainty*, he challenged the modern tendency to inscribe matters of certainty within the same "queer" or "occult" domain. To this tendency, Wittgenstein responded, "Forget this transcendent certainty, which is connected with your concept of spirit."[38] Such "transcendent certainty" is "how our *imagination* presents knowledge" due to the way modern philosophy privileges thought over practice, but this imaginative picture of certainty is not what actually "lies at the bottom" of the matter.[39] The bottom level of certainty, instead, exists at the level of practice. Certainty depends upon the ability to "give grounds" when one's way of thinking and acting is called into question—this much is true. "But the end is not an ungrounded *presupposition*" which must hold apodictically firm but "an ungrounded way of *acting*."[40]

When seen in this light, the legs are taken out from under skepticism because "the game of doubting itself presupposes certainty,"[41] which is, in turn, founded upon such "ungrounded ways of acting." But even more important than short circuiting the skeptic, understanding the final grounds of belief and practice in this way exposes the myriad of certainties that a person always already operates with at pre-theoretical level. Holmer summarized well what Wittgenstein was getting at in *On Certainty*:

> There are all kinds of certainties that give a kind of framework to my action, thinking, feeling, and without which I simply could not make any sense at all. These certainties—and there are many more—are usually not taught us in any obvious way. To have them drawn to one's attention is only to discover that one cannot doubt them at all. On the other hand, one does not quite believe them in any active sense either. At least, they are so certain that they seem to be part of the framework and the skeleton of our whole way of living.[42]

In other words, try as we might, thought cannot ultimately ground a way of life because a way of life is always at the ground level of thought. When understood in this light, apodictic certainty anchored by epistemology is seen to be nothing more than muddled thinking. Therefore, Holmer argues, the crisis of certainty that so many religious people face in the world today must be resolved in the same way as the crisis of meaning in Christian theology. Certainty cannot be rebuilt upon an epistemic edifice, because such an edifice cannot hold itself up apart from concrete forms of life. This makes as little philosophical sense as "picking oneself up by one's own bootstraps" makes sense in the language-game of physics. Rather, certainty must be restored by reviving thick Christian practice.

In "Learning to Theologise," Paul Holmer explains that modern Christians have become "deluded by the idea of evidence being necessary for all beliefs."[43] We have been suckered into thinking that there are spheres of inquiry, such as science or philosophy, that are *not* grounded in the pre-theoretical certainties of a certain kind of practice. Thus, in order for theology to stand firm, it must latch onto one such epistemic foundation. However, as Holmer puts it, "Every human activity, including science itself, rests on certainties or beliefs that authorize the whole endeavor. And the foundations themselves have no foundations—they simply are."[44] Seeking to ground theology upon "facts" or "being" therefore turns out to be nothing more than seeking to ground one epistemically ungroundable language-game (theology) upon another epistemically ungroundable language-game (science or philosophy).

The standing of scientific claims seem so certain to modern people, not because they escape the contingencies of human practice, but because the practices of a scientific form of life are taken for granted by most modern people. Theology, similarly, can only reclaim the kind of certainty it seeks by recovering and fostering Christian forms of life and practice which themselves, in turn, will make Christian beliefs "look certain to us."[45]

Conclusion

Throughout this paper, I have aimed to demonstrate how Paul Holmer faithfully projects a Wittgensteinian philosophical method into modern Christian theology through his criticism of modern theology's quest for theistic philosophical foundations, his turn toward an understanding of theology as a "grammar" of Christian life and faith, his insistence that theology requires ethical transformation, and his reevaluation of the question of certainty. Holmer certainly moves beyond Wittgenstein's own limited (though passionate and persistent) reflections on religion and theology. But I believe that Holmer had internalized Wittgenstein's thought to such an extent that he acquired sufficient tacit knowledge to "go on" and extend Wittgenstein's philosophical method to an intellectual arena that was beyond Wittgenstein's area of expertise.

This is not to say that I think Holmer has finished the job. There is more work to be done. In particular, I wish that Holmer had interacted with Wittgenstein's work on aspect-seeing, aspect-dawning, and aspect-blindness. The objective of Holmer's work, however, was primarily to offer a view of theology-as-grammar as an alternative to the predominant and problematic view of theology-as-superstructure-erected-upon-the-foundation-of-theism. In this, Holmer succeeded. And hopefully, his success will inspire successors to further explore the ways in which the thought of Ludwig Wittgenstein might be brought into conversation with contemporary theology.

Notes

1 Ludwig Wittgenstein, *Philosophical Investigations (The German Text, with a Revised English Translation): Third Edition*, trans. G. E. M. Anscombe (Malden: Blackwell, 2001), §373.

2 Wittgenstein's persistent ambivalence to theology is captured in a remark he once made to Maurice O'Connor Drury: "I am not a religious man but I cannot help seeing every problem from a religious point of view." See John Hayes, ed., *The Selected Writings of Maurice O'Connor Drury: On Wittgenstein, Philosophy, Religion and Psychiatry* (Broadway: Bloomsbury, 2019), 151.

3 For a brief overview of the life and work of Paul Holmer on the occasion of his retirement from Yale Divinity School, see Mark Horst, "Disciplined by Theology: A Profile of Paul Holmer," *The Christian Century*, October 12, 1988, 891–5.

4 Three other essays that Holmer wrote on Wittgenstein have been gathered together as part two of the second volume of a recent collection of his papers. Paul L. Holmer, *The Paul L. Holmer Papers*

Volume Two: Thinking the Faith with Passions, ed. David J. Gouwens and Lee C. Barrett III (Eugene: Cascade, 2012).

5 Wittgenstein, *Philosophical Investigations*, §309.

6 Ludwig Wittgenstein, *Culture and Value: A Selection from the Posthumous Remains (Revised Edition)*, ed. G. H. von Wright, trans. Peter Winch, and revised by Alois Pichler (Malden: Blackwell, 2006), MS 112 46:14.10.1931.

7 Wittgenstein, *Philosophical Investigations*, §§115– 16.

8 See chapters 2 and 3 of Ray Monk, *The Duty of Genius* (New York: Penguin, 1990), 28–61.

9 Wittgenstein, *Philosophical Investigations*, §55.

10 Ibid., §43.

11 Wittgenstein would eventually develop the epistemological implications of this line of thinking, observing that "giving grounds, however, justifying the evidence, comes to an end;—but the end is not certain propositions' striking us immediately as true, i.e. it is not a kind of seeing on our part; it is our *acting*, which lies at the bottom of the language-game." Ludwig Wittgenstein, *On Certainty*, ed. G. E. M. Anscombe and G. H. von Wright, trans. Denis Paul and G. E. M. Anscombe (New York: Harper, 1969), §204.

12 Wittgenstein, *Philosophical Investigations*, 171.

13 Paul L. Holmer, *The Grammar of Faith* (New York: Harper & Row, 1978), 54.

14 Ibid., 55.

15 "Theologians who began to cast about for something upon which they could base the theological teachings, tie them all down, show how they start perhaps and how they mean (for all of these different things get lumped together in the search for 'foundations') are frequently led to 'being' and the concept of 'being.' Ontology seems to be a general way to show that what the theologian is talking about really does, after all, refer to something." Holmer, *The Grammar of Faith*, 90–1.

16 Holmer, *The Grammar of Faith*, 91–3.

17 Ibid., 97.

18 Ibid., 102.

19 Ibid.

20 Ibid., 159–60.

21 Of course, as Holmer notes in an essay on tricky questions in the field of epistemology, when a philosopher resists the temptation to "ground" their most basic beliefs and practices in a metaphysical or empirical super-language, they are often accused of being "idealists, realists, materialists, scholastics, or metaphysical skeptics" because many philosophers (and theologians) assume a metaphysical position to be "inescapable." Hence if they are not "realists" in a metaphysical (i.e., "empiricist") sense, they are assumed to be anti-realists, idealists, skeptics, etc. Following Wittgenstein and other "non-systematic thinkers," however, Holmer is trying to challenge the very notion that a metaphysical mode of philosophizing is inevitable and inescapable. Paul Homer, "Some Epistemological Questions" in *The Paul L. Holmer Papers Volume I: On Kierkegaard and the Truth*, ed. David J. Gouwens and Lee C. Barrett III (Eugene: Cascade, 2012), 158–9. Trying to pigeonhole nonsystematic thinkers in a negative systematic category is the final strategy of the theist to subsume all philosophy within the quest for a universal meta-language. Holmer, however, has joined Wittgenstein on his quest for a realism without empiricism—that is, a nonsystematic and nonmetaphysical realism. See Ludwig Wittgenstein, *Remarks on the Foundations of Mathematics: Revised Edition*, ed. G. H. von Wright, R. Rhees, and G. E. M. Anscombe, trans. G. E. M. Anscombe (Cambridge: The MIT Press, 1983), pt. VI, §23.

22 "The confusions which occupy us arise when language is like an engine idling, not when it is doing work." Wittgenstein, *Philosophical Investigations*, §132.

23 Wittgenstein, *Philosophical Investigations*, §53–5.

24 Ibid., §355–73.

25 Ibid., §23.

26 Ibid., §11.

27 Holmer, *The Grammar of Faith*, 118.

28 Ibid., 126–7.

29 Ibid., 128.

30 Ibid., 129.

31 Ibid., 131.

32 Wittgenstein, *Culture and Value*, MS 112 46:14.10.1931.

33 Hence, Wittgenstein notes, people must learn how to apply any such abstractions rightly. Wittgenstein, *Philosophical Investigations*, 193.

34 It should come as no surprise, then, that Holmer also passionately argued for "a rehabilitation of the vice-virtue conceptual language." Modern philosophy tends to put such considerations on the back-burner in order to prioritize issues of "general epistemology." But, along with Wittgenstein, Holmer understands general philosophical principles to be only as good as the person who must make use of and apply them. Paul L. Holmer, "The Case for the Virtues," in *The Paul L. Holmer Volume Two: Thinking the Faith with Passion*, ed. David J. Gouwens and Lee C. Barrett III (Eugene: Cascade, 2012), 306.

35 Holmer, *The Grammar of Faith*, 130.

36 Ibid., 202.

37 Ludwig Wittgenstein, *Preliminary Studies for the "Philosophical Investigations:" Generally Known as the Blue and Brown Books* (New York: Harper, 1960), 5.

38 Wittgenstein, *On Certainty*, §47.

39 Ibid., §90.

40 Italics added for emphasis. Ibid., §110.

41 Ibid., §115.

42 Paul L. Holmer, "Learning to Theologise," in *Wittgenstein: Attention to Particulars: Essays in Honour of Rush Rhees (1905–89)*, ed. D.Z. Phillips (New York: St. Martin's Press, 1989), 195.

43 Ibid., 199.

44 Ibid. In another article entitled "Wittgenstein and Kierkegaard," Holmer clarifies his Wittgensteinian view of how certain "forms of life" act as the basic "givens" of reflection that allow for intersubjective agreement yet avoid the snares of foundationalist epistemology. He writes: "Wittgenstein has effected a change in the use of the word 'given.' For agreement between different persons and understanding something that was said, perhaps some time ago, does call for there being something in common between us. And it has been typical to say experience, sense data, or the 'undifferentiated perceptual field,' was our common starting point, as if that were what was given. But Wittgenstein will have us think differently about what permits agreement and understanding. The ordinary way of thinking about noetic experience or about 'knowing' is being side-stepped. Because he is trying to *describe* the way we actually do come to understand one another and not to idealize or to reconstruct knowing, he says that the agreement point is neither something like a raw datum nor is it an opinion, but it is in the form of life, those describable ways of acting that form our lives."

Paul L. Holmer, "Wittgenstein and Kierkegaard," in *The Paul L. Holmer Volume Two: Thinking the Faith with Passion*, ed. David J. Gouwens and Lee C. Barrett III (Eugene: Cascade, 2012), 80.

45 Holmer, "Learning to Theologise," 199.

6

Theology as Theosis

Terrance Klein

What is the relationship between theology and preaching? Is Christian theology an evolving, rational explication of the data of revelation, patterned according to the philosophic presuppositions of a given culture? Is it an intellectual discipline located primarily within the confines of the academy, one practiced by professors and their students? As such, does it eschew emotive and aesthetic concerns in favor of a rationality that can be translated into idioms that are at least comprehensible, if not actually accepted, by those who pursue other disciplines? In contrast, is preaching only per chance an intellectual engagement with the Christian tradition, a pastoral craft directed toward strengthening the faith of believers, relying upon emotive and aesthetic elements for whatever success it achieves?

Of course when dichotomies are drawn too distinctly, the savvy reader braces to see the division assailed, which is precisely my intent. As I see it, the very existence of preaching, as a properly Christian act, is itself a datum demanding theological reflection. Why do Christians preach? What makes preaching a necessary part of the Christian faith?

After considering preaching as an essential phenomenon of Christianity, I want to argue that a Christian theology, drained of a preaching character, loses a constitutive quality of evangelical witness. Conversely, preaching drained of theology becomes propaganda, because it no longer invites the hearer to see and to believe (cf. Jn 20:8). The physical sight, of which the gospel speaks, includes intellectual insight, a comprehension that comes from contemplation. So the theological nature of preaching is an ongoing task, but it is also a different essay.

Certainly theology and preaching are distinctive fora, but they share a similar noetic orientation, especially when contrasted with religious studies, as those are pursued in the modern American research university. Both theology and preaching exist in order to enable a personal knowledge of, a relationship with, Jesus Christ. To illustrate all of this, I will argue that the mistaken approach of some theologians to the issue of interreligious dialogue—treating Christianity as an object to be studied rather than a personal encounter with the numinous—provides an apt illustration of what happens when theology loses its moorings in the existential act faith, when it is no longer oriented toward that act. I believe that I am on the side of the ages.

Woe Betide Me

Before the rise of universities in the high middle ages, most of Christian theology was a preached theology, so much so that one would have been hard pressed to distinguish between the two. Theological writing was prepared and presented to call and equip people for an act of faith in the Father of Jesus, an encounter with the numinous presence of Christ, as mediated by the Holy Spirit. The triune God used Christian discourse itself as an occasion of grace. Christians were compelled to preach, because they understood their words as mediating the Incarnate Word. On this point, the preface of the First Letter of Saint John provides a concise charter of what it means to be a Christian: it is to give witness to the Divine Word by means of the human word.

> We declare to you what was from the beginning, what we have heard, what we have seen with our eyes, what we have looked at and touched with our hands, concerning the word of life—this life was revealed and we have seen it and testify to it, and declare to you the eternal life that was with the Father and was revealed to us—we declare to you what we have seen and heard so that you also may have fellowship with us; and truly our fellowship is with the Father and with his Son Jesus Christ. We are writing these things so that our joy may be complete. (Jn 1-4)[1]

Indeed the first Christian theologian, who predates the evangelists themselves, was the missionary preacher Paul. "If I proclaim the gospel, this gives me no ground for boasting, for an obligation is laid on me, and woe betide me if I do not proclaim the gospel!" (1 Cor 9: 16). Unlike later Patristic authors, we don't possess transcripts of his homilies, but his letters were clearly intended to be read orally before a congregation, to be a form of personal presence in his absence. With the exception of *Romans*, Paul's letters were typically theology done ad hoc, directed toward calming a pastoral concern and, sometimes, a crisis. Yet the Church quickly came to see them as mediating more than Paul himself. His writings became encounters with the Lord who had inspired them.

The gospels, which postdate Paul, themselves were composed for liturgical proclamation. Before the printing press, very few believers would have individually read them, either as aids to personal piety or as fodder for theological speculation. Congregations would have solemnly heard, "Whoever listens to you listens to me, and whoever rejects you rejects me, and whoever rejects me rejects the one who sent me (Lk 10:16)."

Patristic theology was likewise, in large measure, a preached theology. One can easily enumerate the exceptions, such as the *Didache*, which functioned as a church order, or the writings of Justin Martyr, which were texts to be read and studied by individuals outside the faith, or the work of Origen's catechetical school, which conformed to the Hellenic pattern of master and disciples. But the few exceptions establish the rule. Indeed, before the advent of the printing press, even monastic texts were more likely to be heard orally, rather than read individually. The exigencies of supply and demand necessitated as much.

In characterizing apostolic and patristic theology as preached theologies, I should add that the issue is more than whether or not a text was initially penned for oral presentation, or even that the reception of the text tended to be oral and communal rather than the private perusal of an individual. Early theology was also a preached theology in its dynamism and focus, and it is that exhortatory quality of early Christian theology that I want to focus upon. It called people to a deeper faith.

Learning from Wittgenstein and Kierkegaard

Throughout his long career Paul Holmer, a philosopher of religion, rather than a preacher, wrote frequently on the nature of the theological enterprise, most notably in his extraordinarily useful *The Grammar of Faith,* a work that should still be read by graduate students in theology. Steeped in the writings of Kierkegaard and Wittgenstein, Holmer urged for theology something akin to what the Cambridge don recommended to philosophy, namely, to return words to their ordinary usage in concrete forms of life. For Holmer and theology, that meant systematic reflection upon the act of the faith—the personal bestowal of the individual to Christ—in order to aid the act itself. For Wittgenstein and philosophy, it meant the struggle to free the discipline from the bewitchment that speculation, ungrounded in life as it is actually lived, produced.

Here's how Wittgenstein put the matter in the *Philosophical Investigations.*

> It is not our aim to refine or complete the system of rules for the use of our words in unheard-of ways.
>
> For the clarity that we are aiming at is indeed *complete* clarity But this simply means that the philosophical problems should *completely* disappear.
>
> The real discovery is the one that makes me capable of stopping doing philosophy when I want to.—The one that gives philosophy peace, so that it is no longer tormented by questions which bring in question.—Instead, we now demonstrate a method, by examples; and the series of examples can be broken off.—Problems are solved (difficulties eliminated), not a *single* problem.
>
> There is not a philosophical method, though there are indeed methods, like different therapies.
>
> (§ 133)

Note that, contrary to centuries of the craft's practice, Wittgenstein did not see philosophy as the elaboration of a conceptual system. Indeed the "clarity" that he sought for the discipline had to be existential before it could produce conceptual clarity. As Wittgenstein saw it, perhaps a bit too stridently, philosophical problems disappear when one eschews the conceptual obfuscation that words, distilled from the praxis of ordinary life, can produce. But in seeking to return words to their roots in lived usage, Wittgenstein was doing more than proposing something like a common-sense approach to the perplexities of philosophy. The "therapy" was more radical than that. Philosophy was supposed to make one a better person, and this was to be accomplished by eschewing a rationality alienated from its existential moorings. As Holmer encapsulated Wittgenstein's diagnosis of the discipline, "Where once men philosophized in order to become wise, now, after centuries of philosophizing, the quest for wisdom gets lost in trying to keep the philosophies straight."[2]

Having started with too sharp a dichotomy, I might now be suspected of melding (muddling?) two typically distinct realms, the intellectual and the moral, but a close reading of Wittgenstein's life illustrates the intermingling. At age fifty-eight, Wittgenstein abandoned academia, becoming something of hermit. In large measure the decision was based upon his perception that the modern academic milieu tended to disassociate right thinking from right living. Wittgenstein saw the two as symbiotic. Christianity, of course, does as well.

This vital link between living and learning lay in the very spirit of Søren Kierkegaard, one of the few philosophers whom Wittgenstein himself read and upon whom Paul Holmer wrote extensively. Indeed to read Holmer is to expect that the progenitor of Anglo-American linguistic analysis will be frequently invoked alongside the proto-existentialist Dane. What united these disparate thinkers for Holmer was precisely their insistence that reflection not be sundered from the reality of one's moral life. I could just as well have written, from one's spiritual life. That's the point. For these three thinkers, each was an inextricable part of the whole. "Unlike modern analytic philosophers, who have quite forgotten that philosophy was an activity to Wittgenstein and not a matter of holding analytic doctrines, so too with Kierkegaard. He thought that a philosopher would be a man who would use what he knew ('conceptually' let us say) to stay appropriate to the human task, and the task requires a never-ending striving."[3] All three were convinced that one should think and write as a way to live life, not because one earned an academic's pay, but because thinking and writing exist to purify and to heal human life.

Kierkegaard, of course, was never an academic, nor was he ordained to preach, though he remains among those most frequently quoted in Christian sermons. It's easy to see why. He continually asks the reader to think about life, not conceptually, but ethically. In the well-known words of Kierkegaard's *Journals:*

> What I really need is to get clear about *what I am to do*, not what I must know, except in the way knowledge must precede all action. It is a question of understanding my destiny, of seeing what the Deity really wants *me* to do; the thing is to find a truth which is truth *for me*, to find *the idea for which I am willing to live and die*. And what use here would it be if I were to discover a so-called objective truth, or if I worked my way through the philosophers' systems and were able to call them all to account on request, point out inconsistencies in every single circle? And what use here would it be to be able to work out a theory of the state, and put all the pieces from so many places into one whole, construct a world which, again, I myself did not inhabit but merely held up for others to see? What use would it be to be able to propound the meaning of Christianity, to explain many separate facts, if it had no deeper meaning for myself and for *my life?*[4]

For the Dane, philosophy, especially the sort exemplified by the master-system builder Hegel, only alienated the human person from his or her self. It laid out the entire world in something of a conceptual map, while it left the human person, the one holding the schema, without a word of advice, or consolation, in the face of a life that still had to be lived.

Theology as Theosis

With Wittgenstein and Kierkegaard as the two thinkers whom Paul Holmer read most deeply or, better, the souls with whom he chose to commune, it shouldn't be surprising that, turning to the nature of theology, Holmer would likewise argue that a theology which failed to engage a life of faith failed at the very task of being theology, which is "the means to the understanding, not the understanding itself."[5] Theology is a means; faith in God is the terminus, with faith being understood as a form of understanding and an assent to it, or, put another way, as a personal knowledge of another that emerges from mutual self-bestowal. Here is Holmer's explication:

> Theology, in the wide sense alluded to, is a technical and truly professional enterprise. But in most of what passes as theological study, one never even approximates the essence of Christianity, let alone the knowledge of God. Getting to know the grammar of faith is another matter altogether. Here the skills are also typically indigenous to the educated, plus there is one other factor: a firsthand acquaintance with the form of life that makes a person a Christian.[6]

Consider what Holmer aptly calls "the grammar of faith." The world of the human person is woven of words, because we never step beyond the world that we encounter by means of language. Put another way, because the corporeal intellect that is the human person is linguistic, the act of personal bestowal will have a cognitive, even an intellectual dimension. Hence, far from being superfluous to the act of faith, or detracting from it, theology still serves a vital purpose: it is a manifestation of faith, a necessary, constitutive articulation of it in language. "The language of faith is not *about* the faith—it becomes another instance *of* faith."[7]

One can put the matter even more strongly. Like his forebears in the ancient Church, Holmer insisted that theology, at its core, was a way of living the faith, a form of *theosis* or divinization—to use the Latin term. One doesn't have faith and then choose whether or not to theologize. The self-understanding of the act of faith is necessarily linguistic. It never exists without some form of articulation, however inchoate or limited. Holmer writes:

> If theology is like a grammar, and certainly it is, then it follows that learning theology is not an end in itself. I am not denying here that theology can be learned just as grammar and logic can; most particularly, it is perfectly proper to do so. But there is the additional difference about theology that, though it is like grammar in some respects, namely, in not being the aim

and intent of belief and the substance in and of itself (i.e., in not being the end but the means), still it is the declaration of the essence of Christianity. In so far as Christianity can be "said" at all, theology and Scripture say it. But what is therein said, be it words of eternal life, be it creeds, or be it the words of Jesus Himself, we must note that like grammar and logic, their aim is not that we repeat the words. Theology must be absorbed, and when it is, the hearer is supposed to become Godly.[8]

Theology should draw us into God. Its goal is to make us Godlike. A theology that fails to do this, fails to be theology. It may well be some sort of conceptualization of Christian ideas, but, on the issue of faith, it's essentially a concatenation of words without any rooting in Christ, the one whom Saint John first identified as the Word. Therefore, "the whole thrust of theology has to be in the direction not of finding something out—for that is only at the beginning—but rather of becoming something more worthy and justified."[9]

Of course this doesn't mean that would-be theologians need not spend their time in libraries, that they can confine themselves to chapels. Sadly, being a saint is not sufficient for being a theologian any more than being a theologian makes one a saint. Pope John Paul II aptly spoke of faith and reason as "two wings on which the human spirit rises to the contemplation of truth; and God has placed in the human heart a desire to know the truth—in a word, to know himself—so that, by knowing and loving God, men and women may also come to the fullness of truth about themselves."[10] Many theologians have been saints, but not all saints are theologians, despite their deep grounding in Christ, their existential knowledge of him. A theologian is someone who can use human words, and the conceptual skeins woven of them, to summon men and women to Christ. Therefore, at the very least, a theologian must marshal human words in a manner that makes sense to other humans.

Here those schooled in Karl Barth might object that I have given theology a modernist agenda, that I am reducing the absolutely alien into nothing more than a contemporary believer's buy-in of whatever philosophical system is currently marketable. They would insist that God's word is truly transcendent, that it judges all human words and is not judged by them. And yet, *pace* Barth, a word that would be utterly alien to human-kind cannot be a word of revelation, for the very fact that, if it were as utterly transcendent as to be incomprehensible, it could not be received by humans. To adapt the famous conclusion of Wittgenstein's *Tractatus,* we necessarily would be utterly silent about such a word, because we would know nothing of it. The Word had to become flesh to be received as revelation, which is to say that the revelation that is Christ had entered into the matrix that is human life. A word that would be unrelated to anything within the world would not be divine revelation. It would be literally unintelligible, and an unintelligible word is not revelation.

At first sight, it can appear that Holmer rejects philosophy and the theologies built upon it, because he eschews rationality for fideism, but the target is an existentially disengaged way of doing philosophy and theology. "Oddly enough, Barthians, Kierkegaardians, and Wittgensteinians together look like the opponents of cognitivity and rationality in religion, but only if a certain pattern of rationality is taken to be normative."[11]

> What God is, then, can never be answered by those who read and run. "Tell me 'how' you seek and I will tell you 'what' you are seeking," says Wittgenstein. "If with all your heart, ye truly seek me, ye shall ever surely find me;" that is reported in Scripture as a saying of the Lord. Knowing God, then, is a matter of coming to the religious life. Theology, now thinking of it in the grammatical sense, is not a substitute for worship; and it certainly is not a lofty and sophisticated way to acknowledge God in contrast to the vulgar modes of belief and submissive respect. It does not substitute new concepts for those in the story, for that again is no improvement but is invariably a radically different replacement. One might say that a new concept usually changes the entire grammar. Theology is a name, then, for the ruled way, the correct way, of speaking about and worshiping God. Like grammar in more

mundane instances of everyday speech, theology is both all (204) that we have—namely, knowing what is right to say—and also the way one secures the identity of God. So we do not know the true God or know God truly by a simple use of the word *God*. The true God is known only when his identity is established in a tradition and ruled by practice of language and worship. This is the grammar, the theology, provides.[12]

Even proclaimed and published words—sacred scripture itself—can be unrevealing words precisely because one does not encounter the living God by means of them, either because one is entirely ignorant of them, or because conceptual and intellectual prejudices prevent one from receiving these words as revelation. Hence the mediating task of the theologian. "The language of faith brings us much closer to the actual knowledge of God. Notwithstanding, that language of faith still does not impart knowledge of God directly."[13] Holmer writes that "the language of faith is found paradigmatically chiefly in the Christian Scriptures and the liturgy, but also in less exalted forms in the mouths of the saints and believers through human history. That language can be assimilated by acts of obedience and a simple kind of following."[14]

Holmer called good preaching "vernacular theology."[15] And he was clear about its defining characteristic. "A sermon is not Christian unless it awakens self-reflection, strengthens resolution, and brings the life of the Christian into actuality."[16] Reversing the trajectory, I want to offer a converse characteristic of theology: one ought to be able to recognize good theology, real theology, by its ability to be preached. Does it move one to prayer? Is one forced, so to speak, to remove one's noetic shoes, because one recognizes the self to be in the presence of the Holy One? That seems to be asking a lot of theology, but it does explain why I long for the day when, professional exigencies met, I can sit in some chapel and read Aquinas's *Summa*.

But, speaking of which, allow me to introduce a *sed contra*. Aren't there parts of the *Summa Theologiae* that are downright tedious? Would anyone ever be moved to prayer in reading them? Does that mean that Saint Thomas only occasionally produced theology? And, if the reader hasn't been moved to prayer, or an act of faith, while reading this essay, does that make it some strange, Calaban-like creature, one that discusses theology without itself managing to be theology?

Perhaps I have made the measure of theology so meanly narrow that even sacred scripture itself could not meet it. After all, there are parts of scripture that even the great Origen could not make truly revelatory, not without turning them into something they simply weren't. But, as Origin would suggest, it's the Spirit, who quickens the flesh of the text to which one must attend. In like manner, one has to examine the Spirit at work in various theological texts in order to know which give life. But let's posit a limiting case. What if one couldn't preach or pray over a single sentence, which a theologian produces. Then I would argue that such a person is not a theologian, because the spirit of the text isn't imbued with the Spirit we call Holy. "For the use of religious language, even the Bible and the hymns, liturgy, and prayers, is part of the business of learning to be religious. This is part of the 'how' of being religious."[17]

Indeed the core of Christianity is that revelation and grace are convertible, or, as the Second Vatican Council put it in *Dei Verbum*, its Dogmatic Constitution on Divine Revelation, the Christ revealed in our midst "is both the mediator and the fullness of all revelation."[18] Grace is the divine bestowal of self, and the medium of that self-bestowal is the person of the Christ, who emerges from the drama, which we call the human world. So what God offers in the Christ is nothing less than the divine self. We have no other source, no other medium, of revelation. All that precedes and follows Christ in history being understood as subsumed by himself as the living center of revelation.

Having received the Christ, Christians cannot help but to see creation itself as a vessel of self-bestowal, and they view all of human history, save sin, as being taken up into the sweep of salvation. Hence, Saint Thomas Aquinas, as a Christian theologian could teach that "*Ens et verum convertuntur*" (*De Veritate* 1.1). Thomas was talking about the meaningfulness of reality as a whole. Truth and being must come together, and ultimately they do so in God, who is the fullness of both. Thomas of course was both a great theologian and a great saint. This is an instance where one can see that what he says about reality—that truth and being come together—is deeply rooted in his own personal experience of God.

Grace and revelation are convertible in the life of every Christian, because—whether in print, in liturgical proclamation, or in the address of another—to encounter the Word of God, if that encounter is efficacious, which is to say graced, is always to encounter the person of the Word, the person who is the Word. Revelation, in the very claim to be revelation, entails an encounter with God. If one doesn't encounter God in revelation—and that is the meaning of the word "grace"—then one hasn't encountered revelation at all. One has simply stumbled upon words.

I've just written, parenthetically in discussing revelation, that encountering God's Word is the meaning of the word "grace." Now let me come at revelation by a consideration of grace. We employ the word grace—the Catholic Catechism defines it as God's life—to designate two affirmations. (1) The human person truly encounters God, yet (2) God remains transcendent. We have truly known God, but we do not know God exhaustively. God does not become an object of human knowledge. Hence we speak of an experience being graced to insist both that we have truly encountered God in that human event and that God remains transcendent, still utterly beyond us. Grace is our way of acknowledging both the immanence and the transcendence of God vis-à-vis human life. This is why grace is always a revelation, because it reveals the person of God, who encounters us. It reveals God. We truly "see" or experience God, but we do not noetically subsume God. Analogously, in a human act of communion the very person of the other is revealed, yet the reality of the one who reveals the self is not exhausted in the act. He or she remains transcendent. We do not completely know them.

Revelation and grace are always convertible in the life of a human being. In the act of realizing that one has been blessed, that one has received, one immediately recognizes the giver who gives the gift. Conversely, the very act of discerning the divine Other arises from the recognition that the boon received has its source in the personhood of God. Thus to be graced is also to receive revelation, to become aware of the presence of God in the life of the believer.

Here one begins to see the essential link between theology and faith. Because the human person in a corporeal intellect in the world, God who is the union of knowing and being, bestows the divine self by means of insight, bestows self to insight, bestows self within insight, with insight being the quintessence of what it means to be a human being. Put another way, because human beings are insight, have been created to be insight, God comes to us as insight. All human beings engage God through insight, and those whom we call theologians simply explicate this encounter, conceptually and systematically connecting it to our comprehension of the world.

A personal illustration might help at this point. Many years ago, while still a seminarian, I learned to spend a good deal of my time in both chapel and library, and I noticed something that at the time seemed quite odd to me. On the basis of my own consolation and desolations, as Saint Ignatius of Loyola would term my emotional experiences, sometimes prayer in chapel was fruitful. Sometimes it wasn't. This, despite the fact that I always went there hoping that it would be. The oddity was that I never went to the library expecting spiritual consolations, and yet there were certain writers—for example, Karl Rahner, Hans Urs Von Balthasar, Romano Guardini, and Henri DeLubac—who had this effect on me. Reading them, I would need pause, while seated at some library table, to savor the presence of God. Revelation and grace were convertible.

Interreligious Dialogue? with Whom? Ourselves?

As a test case of this maxim, examine the question of interreligious dialogue, which has become a major focus in the writings of Christians.[19] I have been arguing that true theology should be capable of being preached, that, at its best, is an encounter with

God, which should lead one to prayer. Much of what is written today, by Christians, about non-Christians, fails that test, and it fails it precisely because it approaches Christian revelation as one among many forms of religious wisdom. Presumably, it does so in the, hopefully high-minded, intention of being gracious. The fatal flaw in this approach is its failure to see that, for a Christian, revelation and grace are convertible. To encounter revelation is to encounter God. It is always an act of personal communion. If I have truly been graced by Christian revelation, which is to say, if it has indeed been a revelation of God for me, I cannot suddenly treat this revelation as though it were a noetic object at my disposal, as nothing more than a skein of concepts. To do so would be akin to falling in love and still being willing to listen to another's entreaties that I should abandon the one whom I love for some other love. Lovers give themselves to one another. They are no longer available to other lovers, at least not upon the same level, not as lovers.

Kierkegaard insisted that religious faith involves the bestowal of the entire person to God. As such, as Holmer never ceased to stress, it could not be anything less than deeply subjective, emotional, even passionate. So when he delineated theology from religious studies he stressed:

> The confusion in religious discourse may be described this way: insisting upon the importance of the cognition of a

(religious) possibility, religious faith becomes confused with cognitive belief: insisting upon the non-cognitive aspect of faith, religious sentences mistakenly are assumed to be non-cognitive. Here, instead, a distinction is drawn. Religious sentences are cognitive but are not religious in virtue of this. As cognitive, since sentences describe the possibility of a religious life and believing these sentences is a neutral cognitive act. But becoming religious is a matter of having a non-cognitive enthusiasm and interest in becoming the possibility that can be cognitively described. To translate the sentences into this non-cognitive and passionate context is to put the sentence to a truly religious use. Thus, both cognition and faith can be delineated in relation to the same sentence, the first being non-religious and dispassionate, the second being religious and passionate. But a possibility that can be objectively known and yet subjectively reduplicated is properly called religious when it is remembered that the stress is upon the latter, the reduplication and becoming, rather than the former, the act of awareness.[20]

If you've grown weary, parsing that very dense previous paragraph, in "Theology and the Emotions," Holmer offers a more lapidary equivalent. "A non-theological Christianity would be Christianity without concepts and that is absurd; a non-emotional Christianity, which is without distinctive pathos, feeling, and affects, is a contradiction in terms."[21]

The problem with a theologian writing as though Christian revelation were one truth among many is that it sets Christianity, and, for that matter, all other religious truths, below the intellect of the one making that assessment. The inner cohesion of religious truth, of the various religious systems, becomes a function of mind's contours. In an effort to be fair, or egalitarian, or accommodating, one surreptitiously makes one's own mindset the measure of all religious truth. Again, an illustration is in order.

Not long ago, I listened as a progressive theologian, at an interreligious conference, spoke of looking forward to sitting around a fire, sharing his "story of God" with the stories of other religious peoples, and, at evening's end, each person would be able to confess that they were all superb tales. But, as Holmer pointed out, "If Muslims and Jews can share the same descriptive language about Judaism, if Christians and non-Christians can share the same awareness about the facts, ideas, and practices that make the Christian faith, there must be something else that makes for their differences."[22] Please Lord! Send Karl Barth back for just a day, because what has become utterly transcendent in this Orwellian 1984 religious parable is not the Godhead but the mind of the one narrating the parable. He finds all the stories to be superb. Even those theologies, which focus upon narrative, can introduce a surreptitious metaphysics, which is alien to the Christian faith, when the human mind is taken to be master of the narratives.

Of course some religions present themselves to be no more, or less, than expressions of ultimate human wisdom, and a corresponding praxis for dealing with the deepest realities of life. They are rightfully open to other wisdoms. But a Muslim or a Jew who tells me that his revelation and my own essentially come down to the same thing, is not being faithful to his own encounter with a living, personal God. People are not convertible. Loving this person is not the same as loving that one. In the end, human loves, like human religions, only come together in the God who underlies it all. Or, Thomas would put it, in God alone *ens et verum convertuntur*. Noetic humility demands that we allow truth to be drawn into God, in God's time. We do not reduce God—and religious discourse—to the level of a conceptual system mastered by us.

Each of the revealed religions has its proper apophatic awareness. We do not exhaust the utterly transcendent God. Remember that to assert that revelation and grace are convertible is also to maintain that revelation does not exhaust God. As grace, revelation is a true encounter with God, and Christians assert that God gives self definitively in the Christ, and yet Christ remains transcendent in both his divinity and his humanity. God never becomes a noetic object of the human mind, and, for that matter, nor does another human being. Neither can be circumscribed; both retain the ability to withdraw, to astound, to elude. Human words never encapsulate either God or another human being. Both remain interlocutors; they remain those who continue to speak. This is why we cannot treat either our relationship to the divine or the human as though that which is truly transcendent is the ever-evolving human intellect.

Yet sadly, much of what passes for theological reflection on interreligious dialogue would never pass as preaching would never draw anyone into prayer. Those listening would realize, even if they could not articulate it, that the human mind is wrapping around its own self rather than encountering one whose very presence opens the soul and gives it life.

When the religions of revelation call us creatures, each is suggesting that we are essentially ordered to something outside ourselves, some purpose, some presence, some love utterly beyond us. When a theologian addresses the question of interreligious dialogue, she cannot minimize the numinous in other traditions, and she cannot forsake her encounter with the numinous in her own.

For Wittgenstein, one could say that language and communion are convertible. Language makes communion with others possible, and language itself arises out of our lived communion with others. This is why communion itself becomes a measure of language's efficacy. Words lose their footing when they are no longer rooted in forms of life. Words are always "addressed," which is to say that we use them to communicate, to enter into communion with other interlocutors. "The language of faith is not *about* the faith—it becomes another instance *of* faith."[23]

An academic addresses other academics so that together they might explicate and explore whatever data lie before them. The data exist as noetic objects. A lover, however, addresses another as a way of being drawn into transcendence. Lovers do not come to each other as data; both are inexhaustible presences. A preacher doesn't ultimately impart conceptual knowledge about some object of investigation. He or she calls to others, invites them, by means of words, to encounter that ancient lover of our souls, the Word. And, as Holmer pointed out, writing on Kierkegaard, Christ as Word of the Father is a historical person, not a conceptual system. Hence the nature of the noetic act is that between person, rather than subject-object.[24] In *Training in Christianity*, Kierkegaard wrote:

> Christ is the truth in such a sense that to *be* the truth is the only true explanation of what truth is. Hence one may ask an Apostle, one may ask a Christian, what truth is, and then the Apostle or the Christian will point to Christ and say, "Behold Him, learn of Him, He was the truth." That is to say, the truth, in the sense in which Christ was the truth, is not a sum of sentences, not a definition of concepts, etc., but a life.

Truth in its very being is not the duplication of being in terms of thought, which yields only the thought of being, merely ensures that the act of thinking shall not be a cobweb of the brain without relation to reality, guaranteeing the validity of thought, that the thing thought actually is, i.e., has validity. No, truth in its very being is the reduplication in me, in thee, in him, so that my, that thy, that his life, approximately, in the striving to attain it, is the very being of truth, is a *life*, as the truth was in Christ, for He was the truth.

And hence, Christianity understood, the truth consists not in knowing the truth but in being the truth.[25]

"Considering Christianity, Kierkegaard finds that it posits a relation to God via the historical. This means that any person who stands in a faith relationship must stand also in an historical relation with Jesus of Nazareth." Yet, Kierkegaard writes:

God as an object cannot be known as object but He exists only to be imitated within one's own subjectivity. This is why Christ is the paradox about which historical knowledge can never provide anything of direct religious import, can never be converted into syllogism, because at once He is one who says, "Come unto Me," and, on the other side, from all the historical records there are, is nothing deserving of such universal attention as he seems to suggest.[26]

In *Grammar of Faith* Holmer astutely employed a fundamental insight of Wittgenstein to theology. The meaning of words is not an object standing beyond them in a nonlinguistic realm that stands surety to them. Rather the meaning of a word is found in its usage. Unfortunately, many theologians have yet, even in the twenty-first century, made the famous "linguistic turn." They still think that "meanings are kinds of events, objects, persons, or things lying behind language and for which language is supposed to stand. Then all of language, very and written, is a symbolic activity, but that is a piece of metaphysics, not a matter of common sense or scientific description."[27]

And if one thinks that meaning lies beyond words, one's words can be considered no more than a wrestling with concepts rather than a true encounter with grace. "For the metaphysically oriented theologians have said that the metaphysical concepts are actually more compelling and meaningful, more the essence and heart of the matter, than the language of hymns, sermons, and Scripture."[28] However,

> the Christian faith is the active transformation of an individual's entire mode of existence in conformity with the object of his interest, the person of Jesus. It is not an object or a thing that can be had regardless of the way in which it is acquired. On the contrary, not being a thing, not being a sentence or a doctrine, it is the way it is acquired. It is not

a propositional truth for this can and must be held in a passionless way. Faith instead is a passion.[29]

The issue is not that religious studies and theology cannot coexist in the modern research university. The issue is the distinctive voice, the intent of each. Religious studies reduce religious phenomenon to anthropological and conceptual systems. Theology always seeks personal appropriation of a living faith, a faith that necessarily expresses itself in words. When theology is practiced in universities, it may look more like the former than the latter, but, if so, it has surely lost its way. It no longer hears the voice of the one who compared his own communion with us in the Church, in its language, to that of his communion with his Father, "I am the good shepherd. I know my own and my own know me, just as the Father knows me and I know the Father" (Jn 10:14-15).

Notes

1 The New Revised Standard Version is used throughout this essay.
2 Paul Holmer, *The Grammar of Faith* (San Francisco: Harper and Row, 1978), 4.
3 Paul L. Holmer, *On Kierkegaard and the Truth*, vol. 1 of *The Paul L. Homer Papers*, ed. David J. Gouwens and Lee C. Barrett III (Eugene, OR: Cascade Books, 2012), 107.

4 Søren Kierkegaard, *Papers and Journals: A Selection*, ed. Alastair Hannay (New York: Penguin Classics, 1996), 32.

5 Paul L. Holmer, "About Understanding and Religious Belief," in *Thinking the Faith with Passion*, vol. 2 of *The Paul L. Holmer Papers*, ed. David J. Gouwens and Lee C. Barrett III (Eugene, OR: Cascade Books, 2012) 199.

6 Holmer, *Grammar of Faith*, 194. Holmer made multiple metaphoric uses of the word *grammar*, all of them based upon Wittgenstein's initial usage. The word always indicated an articulated conceptual skein, though he could speak, as he does here, of the grammar of faith, and also, somewhat unhelpfully if one is seeking a stable use of the metaphor, of theology as a grammatical exposition of faith. It's helpful to know that he distinguished between what he called primary language of faith: scripture, liturgy, and the writings of saints and theology as a second level language. The distinction was drawn between the existential and the conceptual.

7 Ibid., 66.

8 Ibid., 19.

9 Ibid., 28.

10 John Paul II, *Fides et Ratio* (Vatican City State: Libreria Editrice Vaticana, 1998), n. 1.

11 Holmer, *Grammar of Faith*, 184.

12 Ibid., 203–4. The quotation from Wittgenstein is found in *Philosophical Grammar*, ed. R. Rhees, trans. Anthony Kenny (Oxford: Blackwell, 1974) 370.

13 Ibid., 192.

14 Ibid., 192.

15 Ibid., 14.

16 Holmer, *On Kierkegaard and the Truth*, 267.

17 Holmer, *Grammar of Faith*, 130.

18 *Dei Verbum*. Dogmatic Constitution on Divine Revelation. Second Vatican Council. Chapter 1, n. 2., 1965.

19 That Christians, more so than other religious adherents, write about interreligious dialogue, is a phenomenon that deserves investigation. Does the new "interreligious moment" represent the exhaustion of the Christian message, or is dynamism outward toward an enveloping expression of the Christ the Word at the very core of Christianity?

20 Paul Holmer, *The Paul L. Holmer Papers: Thinking the Faith with Passion*, ed. David J. Gouwens and Lee C. Barett III (Cambridge: James Clarke & Co, 2013), "The Nature of Religious Propositions," in *Thinking the Faith with Passion*, 213.

21 Paul Holmer, *The Paul L. Holmer Papers: Thinking the Faith with Passion*, ed. David J. Gouwens and Lee C. Barett III (Cambridge: James Clarke & Co, 2013), "Theology and Emotions," in *Thinking the Faith with Passion*, 228.

22 Holmer, *Grammar of Faith,* 64.

23 Ibid., 66.

24 Holmer, *On Kierkegaard and the Truth*, 280.

25 Soren Kierkegaard, *Training in Christianity*, trans. Walter Lowrie (New York: Vintage Press, 2004) 183–4.

26 Holmer, *On Kierkegaard and the Truth*, 291.

27 Holmer, *Grammar of Faith*, 118.

28 Ibid., 129.

29 Holmer, *On Kierkegaard and the Truth*, 295.

BIBLIOGRAPHY

Buber, Martin. *Ich Und Du*. Leipzig: Reclam Philipp Jun, 1995 [1933].
Cavell, Stanley. *The Claim of Reason: Wittgenstein, Skepticism, Morality, and Tragedy*. New York: Oxford University Press, 1999 [1979].
Clifford, William Kingdon, and Tim Madigan. The Ethics of Belief and Other Essays. [Nachdr.] ed. Great Books in Philosophy. Amherst, NY: Prometheus Books, 2009.
Conant, James, and Cora Diamond. "On Reading the Tractatus Resolutely." In *The Lasting Significance of Wittgenstein's Philosophy*, edited by Max Kölbel and Bernhard Weiss, 46–99. London, New York: Routledge, 2004.
Dayton, Donald W. *Discovering an Evangelical Heritage*. San Francisco, CA: Harper & Row, 1976.
Diamond, Cora. "Does Bismark Have a Beetle in His Box?." In *The New Wittgenstein*, edited by Alice Crary and Rupert Read, 262–92. New York: Routledge, 2000.
Elder, Sean. "Why They're Doing Shakespeare in Prison." *Newsweek* (December 11, 2016).
Frei, Hans. *The Eclipse of Biblical Narrative: A Study in Eighteenth- and Nineteenth-Century Hermeneutics*. New Haven, CT: Yale University Press, 1974.
Hall, Daniel E. "The Guild of Surgeons as a Tradition of Moral Enquiry." *Journal of Medicine and Philosophy* 34 (2011): 114–32.
Holmer, Paul L. "About Being a Person: Kierkegaard's *Fear and Trembling*." In *Thinking the Faith with Passion: Selected Essays*, edited by David J. Gouwers and Lee C. Barrett III, 53–78. Cambridge, UK: James Clark & Co., 2012.
Holmer, Paul. "Contemporary Evangelical Faith: An Assessment and Critique." In *The Evangelicals: What They Believe, Who They Are, Where They Are Changing*, edited by David F. Wells and John D. Woodbridge, 88–115. Grand Rapids, MI: Baker, 1977.

Holmer, Paul. *The Grammar of Faith*. San Francisco, CA: Harper and Row Publishers, 1978.

Holmer, Paul L. *On Kierkegaard and the Truth*. The Paul L. Holmer Papers, edited by David J. Gouwens and Lee C. Barrett III. Cambridge and Eugene, OR: James Clarke & Cascade Books, 2012.

Holmer, Paul L. "Learning to Theologise." In *Wittgenstein: Attention to Particulars: Essays in Honour of Rush Rhees (1905–89)*, edited by D.Z. Phillips, 194–200. New York and Frankfurt am Main: St. Martin's Press and Suhrkamp, 1989.

Holmer, Paul L. "Truth Is Subjectivity: Some Logical Considerations." In *On Kierkegaard and the Truth*, edited by David J. Gouwers and Lee C. Barrett III, 133–57. Cambridge, UK: James Clark & Co., 2012.

Holmer, Paul L. "Wittgenstein and Kierkegaard: The Subjective Thinker." In *Thinking the Faith with Passion: Selected Essays*, edited by David J. Gouwers and Lee C. Barrett III, 79–86. Cambridge, UK: James Clark & Co., 2012.

Illing, Sean. "9 Questions for Neil Degrasse Tyson; the Astrophysicist on Curiosity, Bad Intellectual Habits, and Reading National Review." *Vox* (March 25, 2017). http://www.vox.com/conversatio ns/2017/3/25/14986946/9-questions-neil-degrasse-tyson-science-national-review

Jordan, Clarence. *Cotton Patch Version of Luke and Acts*. Clinton: New Win Publishing, 1969.

Kallenberg, Brad J. "Dynamical Similarity and the Problem of Evil." In *God, Grace and Creation: The Annual Publication of the College Theology Society 2009, Vol. 55*, edited by Philip J. Rossi, 163–83. Maryknoll, NY: Orbis Press, 2010.

Kallenberg, Brad J. "Rethinking Fideism through the Lens of Wittgenstein's Engineering Outlook." *International Journal for the Philosophy of Religion* 71, no. 1 (2012): 55–73.

Kenny, Anthony. *The God of the Philosophers*. Oxford, UK: Clarendon, 1987.

Kierkegaard, Søren. *Purity of Heart Is to Will One Thing; Spiritual Preparation for the Office of Confession*. San Francisco: HarperCollins, 1948 [1847].

Lowrie, Walter. *A Short Life of Kierkegaard*. Princeton, NJ: Princeton University Press, 1942.

Malcolm, Norman. *Ludwig Wittgenstein: A Memoir*. London: Oxford University Press, 1958.

Malcolm, Norman. *Ludwig Wittgenstein: A Memoir with a Biographical Sketch by G. H. Von Wright; Second Edition with Wittgenstein's Letters to Malcolm*. Oxford: Clarendon, 2001 [1958].

Monk, Ray. *Ludwig Wittgenstein: The Duty of Genius*. New York: Viking Penguin, 1990.

Russell, Bertrand. "Appearance and Reality." In *The Problems of Philosophy*, 9–26. London: Oxford University Press, 1959.

Sennett, James F., ed. *The Analytic Theist: An Alvin Plantinga Reader*. Grand Rapids, MI: Eerdmans, 1998.

Smith, Jonathan Z. *Relating Religion*. Chicago and London: The University of Chicago Press, 2004.

Wittgenstein, Ludwig. *The Blue and Brown Books*. New York: Harper and Brothers, 1958.

Wittgenstein, Ludwig. *Culture and Value: A Selection from the Posthumous Remains*, translated by Peter Winch, edited by G. H. von Wright and Heikki Nyman, second edition revised by Alois Pichler Oxford, UK: Basil Blackwell, 1998.

Wittgenstein, Ludwig. *Ludwig Wittgenstein: Public and Private Occasions*. Lanham, MD: Rowman & Littlefield, 2003.

Wittgenstein, Ludwig. *Philosophical Grammar*, translated by Anthony Kenny, edited by Rush Rhees. Berkeley and Los Angeles: University of California Press, 1974.

Wittgenstein, Ludwig. *Philosophical Investigations*, translated by G. E. M. Anscombe, edited by G. E. M. Anscombe and Rush Rhees. New York: Macmillan, 1953.

Wittgenstein, Ludwig. *Remarks on the Foundations of Mathematics*, translated by G. E. M. Anscombe, edited by G. H. von Wright, Rush Rhees and G. E. M. Anscombe. Cambridge, MA and London, UK: MIT Press, 1978.

Wittgenstein, Ludwig. *Wittgenstein's Lectures on the Foundations of Mathematics. Cambridge, 1939: From the Notes of R. G. Bosanquet, Norman Malcolm, Rush Rhees, and Yorick Smythies*, edited by Cora Diamond. Chicago: University of Chicago Press, 1975.

Wittgenstein, Ludwig. *Zettel*, translated by G. E. M. Anscombe, edited by G. E. M. Anscombe and G. H. von Wright. Berkeley and Los Angeles: University of California Press, 1970.

INDEX

abstraction
  conceptual 15–16, 24, 160, 178, 185
  and 9, 175
  of the Good 7, 19–20
  from the individual 29–30
  of theological language 124, 132, 174, 183, 186
aesthetics 18, 30, 145, 197
Aquinas, Thomas 212–14, 220
Aristotle 142–3

Barth, Karl 156–60, 162–3, 209–10, 219
Bauer, Wilhelm 111–12
Bell, Richard H. 128–30
Bible, the
  epistemic foundations for 178
  historicity of 126
  inspiration and infallibility of 26–8
  ongoing learning from 58, 75, 81
  skilled use of 213
  strange new world within 163
  treating as a set of propositions 25–8, 87, 90, 134
  see also scripture
being
  as epistemic foundation 174, 178–9, 190, 192 n.15
  union of knowing and 214–15

Bohlin, Torsten 102, 108, 110–17
Brandes, Georg 109–10, 117
Buber, Martin 41–2

capacity, developing a new vi, 2, 135, 137, 148–51, 162–3
Cavell, Stanley 70–3
certainty
  epistemic quest for 9, 19, 24–5, 188–90
  faith as a new kind of 77, 159 (*see also* conversion)
  grammatical/criterial 25–6, 44–52, 55, 83, 174, 188–91
  impossibility of obtaining 20, 26, 43–4, 83
Clifford, W. K. 48
community 47, 52, 58, 75–6, 83–4. *See also* context
concepts
  correct use of 20, 47, 50, 53–4, 76, 209–10
  clarification of 15–17, 181, 203 (*see also* logical investigation)
  contrasted with passions 20–1 (*see also* intellectual myth, the)
  fluency with 45–6, 56–8, 185–7 (*see also* skill; fluency; capacity, developing a new)

misusing 7, 15–17, 24, 60, 130, 132–5, 177–80, 217–20, 224
projection of 70–4, 82–3
reality 9, 13–14, 16
context
abstraction from 28, 142, 185
meaning as dependent upon 27, 47, 72, 131, 150, 153, 156, 176, 179, 181
projection into different 61, 73, 78
of religious language 159–60, 162, 183
see also community
conversion 56–7, 96 n.42
correspondence. *See* truth, correspondence theory of
criterial vs. symptomatic thinking 49–51, 53–6. *See also* internal relations

Dei Verbum 213
Descartes, René 43
doubt 44, 51, 156, 160, 174, 189
dynamic similarity 80

edification 149
empiricism 24–5, 43–5, 52, 179–80, 194 n.21
ethics, ethical
the need for transformation of 187, 191, 205
the subjectivity of 4, 6–9, 17–22, 23–31
as transcendent 145–6
evidentialism 43, 48, 52, 82, 154, 159, 190, 193 n.11

facts
as epistemic foundation 133, 174, 178–9, 190
the place of in religious discourse 23–6, 88, 133–4, 145–6, 153–6
fideism 187–8, 210
fluency 45–9, 53–9, 75–81, 84–5, 96 n.42. *See also* skill; capacity, developing a new
forms of life
agreement in as basis of grammatical certainty 55, 191, 196 n.44
developing fluency in 84, 96 n.42, 187, 191, 206
imposition of alien 180, 186
language as embedded in 19, 77, 152, 177, 181, 196 n.44, 202, 221–2
foundationalism 22, 90, 132, 154, 175–80, 183–92, 196 n.44

Geismar, Eduard 107, 115
go on, understanding as the ability to 78, 88, 191. *See also* projection
Good, the 6–7, 9, 19–21, 25
Goethe 41–2
grace
communicated through Christian discourse 199
convertibility with revelation 213–17, 220
enabling people to inhabit a new world 75, 96 n.42 (*see also* conversion)

Kierkegaard's Lutheran view
of 112
grammar, grammatical
becoming 57–8, 85 (*see also*
fluency; skill; capacity,
developing a new)
certainty 48, 52, 83
vs. epistemology 7–8
investigation 53, 143, 146 (*see
also* logical investigation)
and participation in forms of
life 47–51, 54, 57, 81, 181,
186–7, 206–8
projection of 59
of religious language 133–4,
155–6
theology as 52–4, 57–60, 85,
89, 171–4, 185–7, 191–2,
210–11, 226 n.6

Hauerwas, Stanley 128–9
Hegel, G. W. F. 144, 205
heuristics 185. *See also* tips
Hume, David 43

idealism 9–10, 19–20, 22, 24, 45,
93–4 n.19, 194 n.21
image of God 41
incommensurability 131, 156–7
indirect communication 143–4,
148
intellectual myth, the 4, 17, 21,
23–7, 30–1
internal relation 45, 77, 93 n.10,
95 n.30, 157–8
interreligious dialogue 198, 216,
219, 221, 227 n.19

Jesus Christ 110
conformity to 58, 81, 224
of history vs. of faith 25,
156–62, 223
persecution for the sake of
187
relationship with 56, 60, 76,
157, 198–9, 209
as revelation 209, 213, 220,
222
as truth 103–4, 222–3
two natures of 112, 220

Kabell, Aage 115
Kant, Immanuel 43, 111
knowing how vs. knowing that
185. *See also* skill; capacity,
the development of

language
arising from from forms of
life 19
constituting the world 41–2,
45, 52, 78, 93 n.10
founded on convention 51
ordinary 132, 174–7, 180–2
picture-theory of 42–3, 64–9,
175
as rule-governed 47
theological 157
totalizing 54
language-game 51, 177. *See also*
form of life
Lewis, C. S. 1–2, 6–7, 10–11,
16–17, 22–3, 29–30
Lindbeck, George 124, 127–8,
168 n.54

Locke, John 11, 43
logical form 46, 152
logical investigation 6–7, 10–12, 22–4. *See also* concepts, clarification of
Luther, Martin 107–8, 112–13, 116

Malcolm, Norman 39–40, 46
mathematics 8–9, 15, 43, 85, 176
metaphysics 15, 25, 184, 187–8, 220, 224
monstrous illusion, the 130, 144
Moore, G. E. 65–6
morality
    ethical theory and 125
    separation of reason from 17, 23–4
    unity of the intellect and 119 n.16, 203–5

numinous, the 198–9, 221

objectivity
    considered in opposition to subjectivity 4–7, 12, 23
    insufficiency of for faith without subjectivity 82–3, 130, 205
    as inextricable from subjectivity 4, 13–19, 27–31, 218
    the quest for complete 5–10, 19–20, 25–9, 152 (*see also* sub specie eternatatis)
    see also intellectual myth, the
Origen 200, 212
ostensive definitions 52–3

paradox 20, 107, 112, 114–16, 223
passions
    as a necessary part of faith 21, 74, 82, 224–5
    reformation of as goal of Christian theology 74, 135, 137, 149, 160, 217–18 (*see also* capacity, the development of new; conversion)
    set in opposition to reason 4, 20–1
Phillips, D. Z. 10, 127–8, 131–4, 164 n.1
physics 13–16, 20, 185, 190
prayer 41–2, 184, 186, 212–13, 216–17, 221
preaching
    interrelation with theology 136
    Kierkegaard on 137–8
    as venturesome 137–53
projection
    different methods of 60–74
    necessity of 38, 41, 59, 86, 91
    obstacles to 87–90
    theological 75–86
    of Wittgenstein's thought into theology 173, 191

reactions, habitual and shared 48–55
realism 9–10, 38, 45, 93–4 n.19, 194 n.21
reality
    concepts 9, 16, 144, 155–6, 179
    interplay between individuals and 13–15, 21, 82–3, 214

objective 3–4, 12, 21, 43, 90
old vs. new 57, 163–4
relation to language 25, 45, 53–4
see also world
reasoning, kinds of. *See* criterial vs. symptomatic thinking
relativism 4, 7, 9–10
revelation 209–21
Roberts, Roberts C. 128
Rudin, Waldemar 102, 108–11, 117
Russell, Bertrand 43–4

sin
　confession of 40, 187
　original 112, 114
Summa Theologiae 212
Saliers, Don 128
Sasse, Herman 26
saying vs. showing 93–4 n.19, 145
science 23, 131, 147, 153, 157–9, 180, 190
scripture
　absolute truth of 25–6
　demythologization of 177, 180
　dissection of 151
　as paradigm of Christian language 211
　projection into 75–7
　reading 40
　see also Bible, the
sermon. *See* preaching
Shanker, Stuart G. 8
skepticism 44, 189
skill 47, 64–8, 73–4, 78–9, 86–7, 185, 206. *See also* fluency; capacity, developing a new

Sraffa, Piero 46
Sub Specie Eternatatis 5
subjectivity
　contrasted with objectivity 4–5, 12, 23
　the necessity of 13–14, 28–31
　participating 4, 13–19, 27–31
　see also truth, as subjectivity
Swenson, David
　Interpretation of Kierkegaard by, 102, 104–8, 113–17
　Something about Kierkegaard, 105, 107, 119 n.10
　Translation of *Works of Love* by, 39–40

Tegmark, Max 8
theism 90, 132, 174, 179–84, 187, 192
theosis 198, 206–16
tips 88. *See also* heuristics
truth
　and being united as one 213–14
　Christ as 103–4, 222–3
　correspondence theory of 38, 44
　the nature of religious 21–31, 132–4, 155–7, 160–1, 219
　the quest for objective 4–10 (*see also* intellectual myth, the)
　as subjectivity 38–9, 76, 82–3, 103, 112, 146, 160, 205

Vico, Giambattista 14

Walsh, Sylvia 128
Whittaker, John H. 128, 160–3
will 10–11, 17
Willimon, William 128, 137, 151, 163
Winch, Peter 161–2
"work on oneself" 40, 174, 185
world
    the external 17, 25, 93–4 n.19, 152
    of the happy man 144–6
    old vs. new 56–9, 75–8, 96 n.42, 135, 163
    the relation between language and 41–5, 64, 78, 86, 94 n.22, 207
    of scripture 27, 75–7, 151, 162–3
    shared 54–6, 84
    see also reality

Zeilinger, Anton 13

www.ingramcontent.com/pod-product-compliance
Lightning Source LLC
Chambersburg PA
CBHW062141300426
44115CB00012BA/1999